D. S. BREWER

CHAUCER

1724

LONGMANS

LONGMANS, GREEN AND CO LTD
48 Grosvenor Street, London W.1

*Associated companies, branches and representatives
throughout the world*

First published 1953
Second Edition by photolithography 1960
Third impression 1961
Fourth impression 1962
Fifth impression 1965
Sixth impression 1967
Seventh impression 1968

PRINTED IN GREAT BRITAIN
BY JOHN DICKENS & CO LTD
NORTHAMPTON

TO MY

MOTHER AND FATHER

PREFACE

I HAVE tried to write this short study of Chaucer's life and works for people with literary tastes but not necessarily with any specialized knowledge. The first five chapters therefore attempt to suggest (rather than to describe) something of the general quality of Chaucer's age, and to note the chief events of Chaucer's early life.

I have, of course, drawn on the vast accumulations of medieval and Chaucerian scholarship for my selection of facts, but it seemed pointless to draw up a list of sources which the general reader does not wish to follow up, and which the specialist either knows already or can find in the usual manuals; so I have contented myself and, I hope, the reader, with a very brief note at the end of the book of some other biographies, and of the chief editions and manuals which map out the wide territory of Chaucer scholarship and criticism. My view of Chaucer differs now here, now there, from various authorities, but my limited space has not allowed controversy. Any reader who may be interested must judge the merits of rival interpretations for himself. When so much of the evidence has perished there must inevitably be some uncertainty. I have tried not to be dogmatic where the facts do not justify it, and in a few cases have brought some new information to bear which I hope may be found useful.

Apart from the written work of others, I owe a heavy debt to those who at school and university have taught me the pleasures to be found in English literature. I have particularly benefited in the last year or two from some valuable conversations with Dr. J. A. W. Bennett of Magdalen College. I am also grateful to various friends and colleagues for useful discussions and references. Not least am I grateful to those to whom this book is dedicated, and to my wife, whose invaluable assistance was given during a very difficult time.

D.S.B. (1953)

NOTE TO SECOND EDITION

For this edition I have substituted a slightly fuller bibliographical note, and could not resist re-writing a paragraph or two on _The Parliament_. But with this exception, although there are one or two other points I should have liked to modify or develop, I have decided to let well alone, only asking the moral and philosophical reader

To vouchen sauf, ther nede is, to correcte.

D.S.B. (1960)

The rapid exhaustion of the first printing of the second edition has enabled me to rewrite some paragraphs on _The Legends of Good Women_ and to add a further note to the Bibliography.

D.S.B. (1961)

CONTENTS

Chapter One

A YOUNG SQUIRE

GEOFFREY CHAUCER makes his first appearance on the stage of history with a characteristic combination of vagueness and sharp outline. He is between twelve and seventeen and smallish, wearing shoes, black and red breeches and a 'paltok', or short cloak, bought in London on 4 April 1357, and costing seven shillings in all, the gift of his lady, the Countess Elizabeth of Ulster.

Quite how old he was: how he came to be page to such a distinguished lady, what the rest of his clothes were like (though one imagines they were smart and gay); and many another question has to remain unanswered, or merely guessed at. The thinness of the separate threads which make up the great tapestry of history is well shown by the series of chances which give us this early glimpse of Chaucer. In 1851 the British Museum acquired some manuscripts from the Earl of Denbigh. When the binding of one of these was examined, the covers were found to be lined with leaves of parchment covered with old writing. There were only two leaves, both damaged. They could, however, be read, except for a few words here and there. Handwriting experts gave the date as mid-fourteenth century. The details were seen to be household accounts. They were numbered from thirty to thirty-three—obviously referring to the years of the king's reign (the normal method of dating then); and therefore they could only refer to the reign of King Edward III (the other fourteenth-century kings had not reigned so long). These two humble tattered bits of dirty parchment therefore came from a household account covering the years 1356 to 1359. Closer study of the details showed that the account was kept for a Countess, who lived usually at Hatfield in Yorkshire; that she was related closely to the Royal Family, and that her husband, the Earl, was still alive. These and other details were shown by historians to prove that the lady was Elizabeth daughter of the powerful Earl of Ulster and wife of Lionel, the third son of Edward III. But all this, while perhaps of interest to the specialists, acquires its richest interest by the mention of a few small gifts of money and clothes to 'Galfridus Chaucer'. There are many other records of the fourteenth century, but there appears to have been only one 'Galfridus' Chaucer about this date, and so this is almost certainly the poet; who thus makes his first appearance as already described. On 20 May 1357 a further item of clothing was bought for him in London costing two shillings, and at Christmas in the same year at Hatfield he was given two shillings and sixpence for 'necessaries'.

At first sight these seem small clues to the planting of those seedlings which were to flower as great English poetry. One of the great difficulties of the biography of Chaucer is that the very idea of the *personality* of a poet was barely emerging in the fourteenth century. The art of biography had not arisen, and it was not till well after Shakespeare's death in 1623 that people began to feel that the life of an author might be of an interest even remotely comparable with the lives of soldiers, princes, saints. However, by good fortune, there are a number of records of Chaucer's life and family which have sur-

vived in rent-rolls, City of London Records, Exchequer
Accounts, and so forth—though these were made
because the family was wealthy and Chaucer an important minor official of the Court—not because he was a
poet. Generations of patient and gifted scholars have
ploughed through these ancient crabbed accounts and
records. We reap where they have sown; but rarely
if ever does Chaucer's own character come out. Almost
all we can know of the 'inner life' must come from
literary sources, guided and checked as far as possible by
external facts. Here, then, is the first fact, and modest
as it seems, it can furnish a good many hints to any one
who wishes to practise a little literary detection. First of
all his age. His clothing seems to have cost less than we
would expect for a grown man. Probably then he was
not yet fully-grown. Another clue comes to our aid
here, for in 1386 Chaucer gave evidence in a famous law-
suit over a dispute about heraldic arms, where he gave
his age as forty years old and upward. In those days before
birth-certificates, several other witnesses, sound and
solid knights and gentlemen, in the same law-suit,
guessed their ages wildly wrong, by ten or even twenty
years; but there is no reason to think that so highly edu-
cated and intelligent a man as Chaucer was so badly out.
Also, he lived till 1400, and sixty was a ripe old age for
the times. All the evidence points to some time between
1340 and 1345 as being the date of his birth, and it is
usual to accept 1340 as convenient. Perhaps a year or two
later would be a better guess, making him a page of the
Countess Elizabeth's household from twelve or thirteen
onwards, which would be about the usual age. Sir
Thomas More, a century later, coming from a rather
similar wealthy middle-class family, went as page to a
noble household at the age of twelve.

Our sight of Chaucer in this princely household is also important for showing us his connection, at his most impressionable age, with all the splendour, elegance and sophistication of Edward III's court—the most magnificent in Europe (and also the most efficiently run). Chaucer's lady, the Countess Elizabeth, travelled about the country a great deal, and probably took Chaucer with her. London, Southampton, Reading, Hatfield, Windsor, Hertford Castle, Anglesey, Liverpool all saw her and her train in those four years, some places several times. State weddings and funerals held at Edward's court, as well as the normal feasts of the year, were duly kept by her, and some of them, surely, if not all, by Chaucer in her train. As her page he helped to serve her at table, and attend her at various ceremonies, according to the strict and elaborate etiquette of a great household, which he would have had to learn. Some slight care would also have been taken of his general education, as well as of his manners. Of course, much of what he learned, of politeness, of good manners, of noble behaviour, (as well, doubtless, as scandalous talk, funny stories like the central incidents of some of the Canterbury Tales) came to him by watching and waiting at table, talking with his fellow pages and the older squires, and so forth. But if he did not already possess the knowledge, the Chaplain would also instruct him in some book-learning, and some music, while it is impossible to imagine him not listening to, or even reading for himself, the current songs and romances, especially the fashionable French ones. French was the language of the Court, and though not his mother's tongue, it must have come as second nature to Chaucer. If he went to school, he had to translate his Latin into French. (That great English king, Edward III, spoke French as his mother's tongue and probably knew please; though as his father did not keep a tavern, Furnivall's delightful daydream of him chatting with the customers must be rejected. But we know well enough the kind of things he learnt.

There were at least three schools in London at the time; St. Paul's (a Grammar school, with an Almonry or song-school as a semi-independent attachment), the Arches (at St. Mary le Bow), and St. Martin's le Grand. To one of these Chaucer may have gone. The hours were long, and the holidays none except the festivals of the Church, which would however, have amounted to at least one day a week. The instruction at such a school may be summed up in one word: Latin. Latin was the language of the Church, and of the country's Administration (which was largely run by clerics). It was the language of the Holy Bible; it was the language of philosophy, and of science; and in it was also the most impressive single body of literature known to the Middle Ages —although the vernacular literature of France was certainly the more fashionable at Court. First, however, at the most elementary level of teaching (which they were supposed to have passed through before they came to a grammar-school), children were taught to read in English the Ave Maria, the Lord's Prayer, and the Creed, with a few psalms. Such might be learnt from a primer which might contain first the alphabet in large and small letters, the exorcism, and the Lord's Prayer, followed by the Ave Maria, the Creed, the Ten Commandments, and the Seven Deadly Sins. The child then learnt to read Latin, often without being able to understand it— though this would no doubt depend to some extent on the teacher. Chaucer gives a very touching picture in his own *Prioress's Tale* of a little boy, who has just started at such a school (the text is slightly modernised):

This little child, his little book learning,
As he sat in the school at his primer,
He *Alma redemptoris* hearde sing,
As children learned their antiphoner;
And as he durst he drew him near' and near',
And hearkened aye the wordes and the note,
Till he the firste verse knew all by rote.

Nought knew he what this Latin was to say,
For he so young and tender was of age,
But on a day his fellow gan he pray,
T'expounden him this song in his language,
Or tell him why this song was in usage,
This prayed he him to construe and declare
Full ofte time upon his knees bare.

His fellow which that elder was than he,
Answered him thus: 'This song I have heard say
Was maked of our blissful lady free
Her to salute, and eke her for to pray
To be our help and succour when we die.
I can no more expound in this matter,
I learne song, I know but small grammar.'

Canterbury Tales, VII, 516–36 (B 1706–26)

However, Chaucer would have learnt his 'grammar' at the Grammar School—grammar meaning something more than at present. Not only did it signify grammar in the modern sense of 'the structure of the language', but also, when this was acquired, much that we would now call 'criticism' of various kinds. The commonest way of starting the actual Latin grammar was for the master to dictate it, and the children to write it down, and learn it off by heart. (This method of learning and of acquiring books was in use even in the University. The extreme shortage of books in the fourteenth century has always to be remembered. Memory had to play a far larger part in all schooling and all scholarship than it need do now. Obviously, Chaucer's memory was one of the best. Nevertheless, the hindrance to accuracy occasioned by an almost complete lack of reference books is nearly impossible for us to imagine. Even a dictionary was not easy to come by, and although there were several etymological vocabularies in circulation, only one of them had an alphabetical arrangement.) As soon as children had acquired some knowledge of Latin an attempt was made, in some schools, to enforce Latin speaking at all times. Whether this was entirely successful or not, probably most of the better pupils at any rate acquired some fluency in speaking Latin. Some simple text-books, such as Aesop's *Fables* were read after the elements of grammar, and then some classical authors, especially parts of Virgil and Ovid. But few classical authors were read thoroughly; apart from Virgil, who was considered to be almost a Christian, they were looked upon with suspicion, and Christian authors were preferred. The extremely pious nature of the educational system is one of its most notable characteristics. This again is noticeable in some Rules for Conduct for the boys of Westminster School, which, although written in the thirteenth century, probably applied in the fourteenth, and were similar to those in other schools.

In the morning let the boys upon rising sign themselves with the holy cross, and let each one say the creed, namely, I believe in God, etc., and the Lord's prayer three times, and the salutation to the Blessed Virgin five times, without shouting and confusion; and if anyone neglects these good things, let him be punished.

Then, after they have made up the beds properly, let them leave their room together quietly, without clattering, and approach the church modestly, and with washed hands, not running, or skipping, or even chattering, or having a row with any person or animal; not carrying bow or staff, or stone in the hand, or touching anything with which another could be harmed; but marching along simply and honestly and with ordered step. . . .

Whether they are standing or sitting in the choir, let them not have their eyes turned aside to the people, but rather toward the altar; not grinning, or chattering, or laughing aloud; not making fun of another if he does not read or sing psalms well; not hitting one another secretly or openly, or answering rudely if they happen to be asked a question by their elders. Those who break these rules will feel the rod without delay. . .

Likewise, if anyone who knows Latin dares to speak English or French with his companion, or with any clerk, for every word he shall have a blow with the rod. . .

Again, whoever at bedtime has torn to pieces the bed of his companions, or hidden the bed clothes, or thrown shoes or pillows from corner to corner, or roused anger, or thrown the school into disorder, shall be severely punished in the morning.[1]

A certain impression of violence is increased by what we can guess of outdoor sports. Here again, there is little direct fourteenth-century evidence. But things changed slowly in the Middle Ages, and boys' games also are largely traditional. So it seems fair to quote a twelfth-century account of some games, since the picture it gives us is indirectly confirmed by what we know or can guess about the fourteenth century.

On holidays all the summer the boys play at archery practice, running, jumping, wrestling, putting the stone, sending missiles attached with thongs beyond a mark, and duelling with bucklers. The girls Cytherea leads in dancing until moonrise, and the earth is beaten with the lively foot.

[1] Quoted by E. Rickert, *Chaucer's World*, Oxford University Press, 1948, pp. 116–17.

In winter on almost all holidays before dinner, foaming boars and pigs armed with gleaming teeth are made to fight for their heads so that they may be added to the flitches of bacon, or fat hooved bulls or huge bears are made to fight with dogs set upon them.

When the great swamp that borders the northern wall of the city is frozen over, crowds of boys go out for fun on the ice. Some take long runs and slide far across toward the other side. Others make themselves seats out of lumps of ice like great stones; and many running ahead, hand in hand, draw the one who is seated thus. With such a slippery speed of movement, sometimes they all lose their balance and fall headlong. Some know how to have [still] better sport on the ice: they fit to their feet and bind about their ankles bones, such as the thigh bones of animals, and take in their hands stakes tipped with iron; when they strike these on the ice, they are carried with the speed of a flying bird or of a dart from a sling. Sometimes from a great distance, by agreement, two advance [in this way] from opposite sides; they come together, they lift their sticks, they strike at one another; one falls or both, not without bodily hurt; for after the fall even, by the very force of the motion they are carried far, and where they strike the ice, they are skinned and bruised. Often the one who falls breaks an arm or leg by falling on it; but youth is eager for glory, youth is greedy for victory, and in order to be the braver in real battles, they practise these mock battles.[1]

Of course, in this general picture of a fourteenth-century childhood we cannot estimate the interests and activities of Chaucer himself as a boy. But here at least is a taste of the atmosphere in which he spent some formative years—an atmosphere of energetic and some-times constricting piety, varied by violent and excitable sports, with fair opportunity for reading. Indeed, if he was connected in any way with the Almonry School at St.

[1] Quoted by E. Rickert, op. cit., p. 227.

Paul's he had access to an unusually varied collection
of books, and in this, or in some similar collection, he
must have read with a passionate interest.

In 1356, or a year or two earlier, Chaucer stepped out
of this schoolboy world, or out of some unknown tutor's
care, into the more sophisticated world of a great lady's
household, where he was probably in public attendance
on the lady herself. It was as if he had entered a new
dimension, that of 'Courtliness'. He did not merely
discover bright pageantry and elaborate manners—he
would already have seen much of both in London, in
school and church. The most notable difference must
have been the new awareness of the whole ethos of
courtly chivalry, i.e. fighting and lovemaking.

The most glowing description of the world of the
court of King Edward comes from Jean Froissart, the
man who, of all men, was most enamoured of the brilliance and romance of fourteenth-century chivalry. Unlike
Chaucer, he was a professional man-of-letters, rewarded
by gifts from patrons and sinecures in the Church. But
his career offers some interesting parallels to that of
Chaucer, who must have known him, and who certainly
copied his verse. Froissart's early days are even more
obscure than Chaucer's. First, we note that in his poetry
he makes three references to his age, and thereby gives
us the choice of three different birth-years—1333, 1337,
1338. Such is the pleasing casualness of the fourteenth
century towards unimportant details. Froissart was a
Fleming, and, like Chaucer, seems to have been born
in a wealthy middle-class family, and to have early moved
in courtly, aristocratic circles—in some respects, as we
see, the social system was not so rigid as is sometimes
thought. He began Latin at twelve, which was later
perhaps, than an English boy would have done. But, he

says with un-Chaucerian complacence, he was more interested in the little girls, and in fighting the other boys,
than in his lessons. In 1362 he came to England, to find
as his patron his fellow-countrywoman, Edward's Queen
Philippa, whose praises he so warmly tells wherever he
finds occasion. The young Froissart, enamoured of
chivalry, was enraptured by the English court, then at the
height of its glory. 'London was a place of delights. "This
splendid and honourable court, this king feared by three
kingdoms, this noble queen", whom he served "with
beautiful ditties and treatises of love", and these knights
"who spoke as they should" inspired limitless admiration
in him—all the enthusiasm of one's twentieth year.'[1]
The English knighthood was at the full flush of its early
splendid successes in the Hundred Years' War. The
court was full of the heroes of both sides, including
Prince Edward, 'the first knight of the world', whom
later ages have called the Black Prince; with his Princess,
Joan, the Fair Maid of Kent, 'the most beautiful woman
in the whole realm of England' says Froissart, 'et la plus
amoureuse', with her strange, rich, new fashions of
dress which the moralists so condemned. It was the most
brilliant moment of Froissart's life, and one he never
forgot. 'I could not tell nor recount in a day the noble
dinners, the suppers, the festivals, the entertainments,
the gifts, the presents, the jewels, which were made,
given and presented' he cries. He was astonished and
delighted by the courtly manners of the English knights.
They had an absolute faith in a knight's word of honour,
such as was never found among the Germans (whose
brutality Froissart had no love for). To the many captured French knights who remained at the English court
awaiting their ransoms and passing the time in sports, and

[1] M. Darmesteter, *Froissart*, Paris, 1894, p. 23.

feasting with their captors, (who spoke the same language), that court was no place of exile and desolation; rather, says Froissart's biographer, was it like some important town today at a time of an international congress. In this court it was Froissart's delight to collect the materials for his great *Chronicles*, to write fashionable verse, and to talk with gallant lords and ladies of those two 'eternal' themes, Arms and Love.

Of course, there was another side to all this. Froissart himself, later in life, said hard (but doubtless well-deserved) things about the English. The Hundred Years' War usually appears to us now as a long-drawn-out horror of pointless desolation and suffering inflicted on the fair land of France and her wretched peasants. Even within the limits of his own chivalric ideal Froissart sees easily enough, and describes clearly enough many instances of bad faith and wanton cruelty. But though much that was said about chivalry in the fourteenth century was doubtless lipservice, the ideal itself was a potent and glittering one, and for all its faults it has enriched the human mind. It was, so to say, the ideological background for most people in the Court, and so, to some extent, for Chaucer. Its genuine power over the actions of men was limited, and often failed completely, as can be easily seen in Froissart's *Chronicles* themselves. But there are also many examples where the ideal did not fail. Perhaps the most striking brief example of the ideal, because of the person who expresses it, and at such a late date, is the sentence which the unhappy and disastrous King Richard II was said to have uttered, when very near the time of his death; 'Je suis loyal chevalier et oncques ne forfiz chevalerie.' Whatever his faults, the king *believed* in the chivalric ideal.

The central myth had already been created—King

Arthur and his Knights of the Round Table. King Edward created its ceremonies when he founded the Order of the Garter at Windsor. Many other similar orders were created in England and in France at that period. And if the 'religion' of chivalry was more honoured in the observance of ceremony than performance of the ideal, it is not alone among religions for that. Its heads may be summed up very briefly: Christianity, Knightly Combat, Love; and its prime virtues were loyalty and courage. In fact, the Christianity, which was nevertheless a genuine part of the whole, seems usually to have been somewhat overshadowed by the interest in Arms and Love. The desire for worldly glory and wealth was substituted for what had once been (though for a very short while) a desire for treasure in heaven. The Christian ideal found its practical expression, if at all, in such simple and genuine piety as that of John of Gaunt, consisting largely in financial, political and military support of the somewhat ramshackle edifice of the late-medieval Church. There was a similar gap between the ideal of Knightly Combat, and the actual practice of the stratagems, tactics, and violent deeds, of war. So too, with Love. On the one hand, ladies were adored, and the love of his lady was considered to be the source of all that was good in a man's thoughts and actions. On the other hand, children were sometimes married for the sake of their property before they were out of the cradle.

Perhaps the happiest and most typical example of fourteenth-century chivalry is to be found in the tournaments. Here are all the splendour and elaborate ceremonial of chivalry and its colourful trappings; Glory, Arms, and War, in their richest combination. In these noble sports we are not shocked by the sight of the sufferings inflicted upon the innocent, and such a general spectacle of futility and misery in human affairs as we must be strongly aware of in any final consideration of, for example, The Hundred Years' War. It was in the tournament, relieved of the insistent pressure of everyday life, and of the ordinary greed of power, money, and land, that the chivalric ideal of the fourteenth century most truly realised itself. There knights fought for glory and the love of their ladies, there true courtesy could most easily and gracefully express itself, with all the glorious panoply of gold, silver, silk, bright armour, and lovely ladies looking on to admire and applaud. Fortunate indeed, one might say, that a century could realize its ideal in even this limited fashion of an afternoon's sport—which was yet bloody enough by modern standards, and often fatal. We too are fortunate in that the tournament, in very conception a work of art, has been so well portrayed in literature. Froissart excels himself in his descriptions, and describes indeed those very jousts in Smithfield in 1390 for which Chaucer, as Clerk of Works, was responsible for erecting the lists. (This difference of function in relation to the same tournament is almost symbolic of the characteristic difference between the two men.) Sir Thomas Malory also, in the *Morte d'Arthur* describes the tournament in noble terms. But certainly, one of the richest, and at the same time most realistic descriptions we have, is, as we might expect, by Chaucer himself, in the *Knight's Tale*, when Palamon and Arcite and their champions come to fight for the love of the bright Emily. The occasion as Chaucer describes it, becomes as vivid as a Saturday afternoon football match (to which indeed, it was the fourteenth-century equivalent) especially with the groups of people

Heere three, ther ten, holdyng hir questioun
Dyvyninge of thise Thebane knyghtes two.
Somme seyden thus, somme seyde "it shal be so";
Somme helden with hym with the blake berd,[1]
Somme with the balled,[2] somme with the thikke-herd.[3]

Canterbury Tales, I (A), 2514–8

Chaucer almost gives us the odds. Froissart never gives us this kind of realism. However, Froissart, one feels, took the basic idea of the tournament more seriously than Chaucer. Chaucer never mocks it in the *Knight's Tale*, but it is a theme somewhat remote, as it never is in Froissart. For it is worth noticing that in fact the romantic reverence of what was in some respects the adolescent ideal of chivalry finds almost no place in Chaucer. He must have accepted it, when a full-grown man, as part of the normal pattern of life. It may well have delighted him as a youth, but no story of truly Arthurian adventure figures in his poetry, and his opinion of the literary merits of the contemporary English romances of chivalry can be easily judged from the satirical mockery of the The Tale of *Sir Thopas*.

Whatever the nature and course of Chaucer's opinion of it Chivalry both ideal and actual was the main distinguishing quality of the brilliant court with which, as a page to the Countess, he frequently came into contact. And he may well have accompanied her when she went to Windsor for the Feast of St. George, as a member of the Order of the Garter. A closer description of the convention of love will be made in the next chapter, when we come to look more closely at the literary influences which moulded the young poet's mind. This chapter

[1] beard.   [2] bald.   [3] thick-haired.

will best be finished by some further indication of Chaucer's experience of the convention and practice of Arms—his soldiering in Flanders—which directly influenced him very little as a poet, but which, though brief, must have added considerably to his picture of life.

When Edward III invaded France in 1359, Chaucer went with the Army, probably in the service of the Countess Elizabeth's husband, the Duke Lionel. It was an expedition so characteristic of the time that it is worth quoting in itself (apart from its interest as a part of Chaucer's experience) for its magnificence and military futility, its combination of noble deeds of chivalry with acts of terrible cruelty and wanton destruction. The king embarked dangerously late in the year, with the most elaborately equipped army that had yet been seen in France. Froissart describes the baggage-train as over two leagues long, and his divisions so richly bedecked 'that it was joy to see them'.

The kynge of Englande and the great men of his oost had ever with theym in their cariages tentes, pavilions, mylles, ovyns, and forges, to syeth and to bake, and to forge shoos for horses; and for other thynges necessary, they had with them a VI. M. cartes, every carte at lest with iiii. good horses brought out of Englande; also they brought in these cartes, certayne botes made of lether, subtilly wrought, and sufficiently every one of them to receyve iii men, to row in water or rivers, and to fysshe in them at their pleasure, the whiche dyd the great lordes moche pleasure in the Lent season. Also the kynge had a xxx. faukoners a horsbacke, with haukes, and a lx. couple of houndes and as many greyhoundes, so that nere every daye eyther he hunted or hauked at the ryver, as it pleased hym: and divers other of the great lordes had houndes and haukes, as well as the kyng. And ever as the ost removed, they went in thre batailes, and every batayle had

his vawarde, and every oost lodged by themselfe, each a
leage from other.

Berners' Froissart, Tudor Translations, 1901, II, p. 51

When such a vast army moved, it ate the surrounding
countryside bare like a swarm of locusts. But also from
this may be seen the elaborate administrative efficiency
which, until guerilla tactics were adopted by the French,
had made the English army, with its new and unchivalrous
weapon, the longbow, so devastating to the French.

The outstanding event of this military promenade
(apart from the desolation it caused which so shocked
Petrarch) was the unsuccessful siege of Rheims.
Chaucer's first campaign was an exceedingly uncomfortable one, for all the equipment the English took.

They had nat all their ease, for they were there in the hert of
wynter, about saynt Andrewes tyde, with great wyndes
and rayne, and their horses yvell lodged and entreated, for
all the countrey, a two or thre yere before, the yerth had not
ben laboured. Wherefore there was no forage to gette
abrode, under x. or xii. leages of, wherby there were many
frayes: somtyme thenglisshmen wan, and somtyme lost . . .
they of the host rode often tymes abrode to fynde some
adventure . . . and wolde lodge out of the host a thre or
foure dayes, and robbe and pylle the countrey without any
resistence, and then agayne repaire to the oost.

Ibid., II, p. 44

Perhaps it was on one of these raids that Geoffrey Chaucer
was taken prisoner; but however it happened, captured
he was.

Two minor episodes will suggest the nature of the
war, neither of them by any means exceptional. The first
well illustrates the wild and irrational violence which
marked the century. Sir John Chandos (one of the

noblest and wisest knights of the time) with Sir James
Audeley, and others (not all English—some were Gas-
cons) came to the castle of what is now Cernay. They
decided to attack it, but it was held by two good knights,
one of them called Gui de Chappes. There was a 'sore
assault' in which one of the attackers, the Lord of
Mucident

> adventured hymselfe so forewarde, that he was stryken on the
> heed with a stone in suche wyse, that there he dyed amonge
> his men, of whose dethe the other knightes were so sore
> displeased, that they sware nat to departe thense, tyll they
> had that castell at theyr pleasure, whereby the assawte
> encreassed; there were many feates of armes done, for the Gas-
> coyns were sore displeased for the dethe of theyr maister
> and capitayne, the lorde of Mucident. They entred into the
> dykes without feare, and came to the walles, and mounted
> up with theyr targes over theyr hedes, and in the mean tyme
> the archars shotte so holly toguyther, that none appered
> withoute he was in great parell; the castell was so sore
> assayled, that at laste it was taken and wonne with losse and
> hurte of many menne. Than the two captaynes were taken
> (i.e. made prisoner) and certayne other squyers, and all the
> residewe slayne withoute mercy, and rased downe, and
> brent as moche as they myght of the castell, bycause they
> wolde nat kepe it; and than retourned to theyr ooste, and
> shewed the kynge what they hadde done.
>
> *Ibid.*, II, p. 45

The other episode is of a very similar incident, which
also occurred during this same siege of Rheims, and
shows the nobility and courtesy with which the war was
sometimes conducted. 'Syr Bartilmew de Bonnes' was
lodged, with his company of spears and archers, near the
strong castle of Comercy. Sir Bartilmew (or Bartholomew) saw he could not take it by assault, and so set a
number of miners at work, paying them good wages.

When they had finished he went to the castle and invited
Sir Henry Devoyr, the captain, to surrender. The captain not unnaturally refused.

> Well, quod syr Bartilmewe, and ye knewe what case ye
> stande in, ye wolde incontinent yelde up withoute any mo
> wordes. Why, quod syr Henry, what case be we in. Issue
> out, quod the Englysshe knyght, and I shall shewe you, and
> ye shall have assurance to entre agayn if ye lyste. Than syr
> Henry, and iiii, with hym, issued out and came to syr Bartil-
> mewe, and to John de Guystelles, and they brought hym to the
> myne, and there shewed hym how the great toure stode
> but on stages of tymbre. Whan the knyght saw the parell
> that he was in and hys company, he sayd, Syr, it is true,
> and this that ye have done to me is of your great gentylness:
> we yelde us to your pleasure. There syr Bartilmewe toke
> them as his prisoners, and made every man to come out of
> the castell, and al theyr goodes, and than he set fyer into the
> myne, and brent (i.e. burned) the stages, and than the
> toure clave asonder and fell to the erthe. Loo, quod sir
> Bartilmewe to sir Henry, beholde nowe yf I said truth or nat.
> Syr, it is true, sayd sir Henry, we are your prisoners at your
> pleasure, and thank you of your courtesye, for yf some other
> had us in this case we shulde nat have been so delte with all.

Ibid., II, pp. 49–50

This was Chaucer's war, though of his personal experience, beyond the bare fact that he was captured, we
know nothing; he never refers to it in any writings which
survive. We know from Exchequer accounts that the
King financed his ransom, either wholly or in part, to the
extent of £16—quite a large sum, though it is by now a
hoary joke that the King paid a trifle more for a favourite
war-horse. Chaucer was released on 1 March 1360, and
returned to England in May. Later in the year he was
still in Duke Lionel's service, as can be told from the
Duke's expense book; and during the peace negotia-

tions he went back to France, on his return carrying
letters from Calais to England. This was perhaps the first
of his many journeys in a position of trust, or he may
simply have acted as a courier.

None of this makes the question of his age any clearer.
The Black Prince commanded his first army and won his
first battle at the age of fourteen. In 1359 Chaucer need
have been no older to take part in a campaign.

This marks, at least to our eyes, a period in his life.
Scanty as the records have been up to date, there is complete silence for the next seven years, though intelligent
guesses, notably by Professor Manly, are not lacking. At
this point we may well sum up what we know of Chaucer
by quoting Chaucer's own description of the Squire in
the Canterbury Tales. Of course, Chaucer was not the
son of a Knight. But he was certainly page and perhaps
squire in one of the greatest households of England. He
had been 'in chivachye' in Flanders, Artois and Picardy;
he certainly was a rhymer; and many young men of his
age have been in love. Chaucer's picture of the Squire
is an idealized one, and in no sense a self-portrait. But
it describes the type of young man superbly well, and
Chaucer must have been such another. We are hardly
likely to get nearer than this:

> a yong Squier,
> A lovyere, and a lusty bacheler,[1]
> With lokkes crulle,[2] as they were leyd in presse.
> Of twenty yeer of age he was, I gesse.
> Of his stature he was of evene lengthe,
> And wonderly delyvere,[3] and of greet strengthe.
> And he hadde been somtyme in chyvachie,
> In Flaundres, in Artoys, and Picardye,
> And born hym weel, as of so litel space,
> In hope to stonden in his lady grace.

Embrouded[4] was he, as it were a meede[5]
Al ful of fresshe floures, whyte and reede.
Syngynge he was, or floytinge, al the day,
He was as fressh as is the month of May.
Short was his gowne, with sleves longe and wide.
Wel koude he sitte on hors, and faire ryde.
He koude songes make and wel endite,[6]
Juste[7] and eek daunce, and weel purtreye[8] and write.
So hoote he lovede, that by nyghtertale[9]
He sleep namoore than dooth a nyghtingale.
Curteis he was, lowely, and servysable,
And carf biforn his fader at the table.

Canterbury Tales, Prol. 79–100

[1] young knight. [2] curled. [3] nimble. [4] embroidered. [5] meadow. [6] write.
[7] joust. [8] draw. [9] night-time.

Chapter Two

THE LITERARY TRADITION—CUPID AND REASON

ALL we know of Chaucer between the autumn of 1360 and 20 June 1367, is that he had married by 12 September 1366, for a lady named Philippa Chaucer received a payment of money on that date. But he must have read continually:

> On bokes for to rede I me delyte
> And in myn herte have hem in reverence
> And to hem yeve[1] swich lust[2] and swich credence[3]
> That there is wel[4] unethe[4] game non
> That fro my bokes make me to gon.[5]
>
> *Legend of Good Women*, Prol. AG. 30–4

Chaucer wrote this late in life, but there is ample evidence that it was always true of him.

Some of his reading was scientific, philosophical, and religious; but most of all at this time he read *Le Roman de la Rose* and modern poets, Machaut, Deschamps and Froissart. These poets were all French (Chaucer rarely displays knowledge of English poets), and they wrote mostly about love at what now seems excessive length. The joys and miseries, the frequent rebuffs, the refinement, nobility, and bravery which only love could inspire were all thoroughly worked over, and, one would have thought, worked out. These poets are not without their charm, but they are artistically in the doldrums. Nevertheless Chaucer loved them; he had much of their

[1] give. [2] pleasure. [3] belief. [4] scarcely at all. [5] go.

writings by heart and imitated or translated many a
fragment from them. It may be that he took the somewhat unusual step of writing in English rather than in
French partly from his desire to imitate them in a fresh
language.[1] Deschamps, at least, was grateful to Chaucer
for such efforts, and wrote him a poem where he praised
him as

> Grand translatcur, noble Geffroy Chaucier.

It is natural that Chaucer's earliest poems should be
imitations like *The Complaint unto Pity*, or translations.
Two of his early translations, *The Romaunt of the Rose* and
An A.B.C., are particularly significant, for they represent
the dominant influences of his youth, the medieval tradition of love, and medieval Christian teaching. They give
us his starting point, intellectually, emotionally, artistically. *The Romaunt of the Rose*, which survives in only
one manuscript, is a fragment of some 7,500 octosyllabic
lines, of which probably only the first 1,705 lines are
Chaucer's. This English *Romaunt* is a translation of parts
of the French *Roman de la Rose*, which was one of the
great formative books of the Middle Ages. More than
two hundred French manuscripts of the *Roman*, besides
translations into other European languages, and twenty-
one early printed editions, bear witness to its enormous
popularity. It was at the well-head of the tradition in
which Machaut, Deschamps and Froissart wrote. And
although Chaucer actually translated very little of its
more than twenty thousand lines, he knew the whole

---

[1] Before printing, when books were scarce, no one thought that copying or
translating was mere plagiarism. There was no sense of 'author's rights', or
even of author's personality. A book was a book and the better the book, the
better it was to reproduce it. To copy a book out oneself, or have a scribe copy
it, was a work of great labour or expense, and an author, if he knew about it,
would be grateful. The author's emoluments came from his patrons or from
some employment unrelated to his writing, whether or not a sinecure.

poem extremely well. It permeated his thought so
deeply that his later works reveal its influence even more
profoundly than his early poems.

The *Roman* was written by two authors as different as
chalk from cheese. Guillaume de Lorris wrote the delightful first part of some four thousand lines, about the year
1225. The poem tells how the narrator fell asleep and
dreamt it was the sweetest of May mornings. Wandering by a clear river, he came to a beautiful Garden 'from
whose walls sorrow flies far', whose lord was Mirth,
and from which everything old, ugly, poor and vicious
was excluded. Within this garden of youthful delights
the Dreamer eventually saw the Rose, and as he looked,
the arrows of Cupid, the god of love, struck him again
and again. But the Rose (a lady's love) was defended by
thorns, by guardians such as Modesty and Rebuff
(*Daunger*). Furthermore, the lady Reason, who had been
created in Paradise by God himself, attempted to dis-
suade the Dreamer from trying to win the Rose at all.

Guillaume did not finish his poem. It was finished
some fifty years later by Jean de Meung, whose nickname,
'Le Clopinel', the Hobbler, not unaptly suggests his
difference from Guillaume. Jean took over the machin-
ery of the poem to convey a great quantity of very various
matter; philosophy, science, nature poetry, controversy
and satire of all kinds, but especially of women. It was
this huge and shapeless addition of Jean's that caused the
Roman to be sometimes cited in the fourteenth century
as a satire against love, notwithstanding its beginning.[1]

The whole poem is encyclopaedic in its range, most
characteristic of the thirteenth century. It set or rein-

[1] Apart from the incomplete Middle English translation there is a modern
translation by F. S. Ellis, in the Temple Classics. C. S. Lewis, *The Allegory
of Love*, has a chapter on the *Roman* and brilliantly treats the whole question
of the love-tradition in medieval literature.

forced the fashion for several important literary tradi-
tions. The device of the dream, the artificially bright
May morning, the lovely Garden representing the youthful view of the gay world, the allegorical framework,
as well as many individual types and comments, all
appear again and again in later poetry. Guillaume's poem
sets out the 'law of love'. His god of love is the medieval
Cupid, no fat, blind, naked infant, but a princely young
hunter of men. The lover receives his code from the god,
and learns that nobility must derive from virtue, not from
lineage; that he must always be faithful; always fashionable though not extravagant in dress; accomplished in
both manly and artistic exercises. In a word, he must
be a gentleman in every respect, with his teeth as un-
stained as his honour. For the practice of these virtues
the lover is promised the highest joys and bitterest sorrows that life can offer.

Even in Guillaume, however, love has an antagonist,
the Lady Reason, who descends from her tower to defend
Chastity and to argue against the dictates of Cupid.
Guillaume makes her arguments seem cold and merely
prudential, and we sympathise with the lover's rejection
of them. But the conflict is deep at the heart of love as
seen by the medieval poets, and it is by no means certain
that Guillaume himself would have been finally on Cupid's
side. The antithesis between the service of love and the
service of God was clear, and always profoundly felt.
There is no doubt that Chaucer also felt it.

Jean de Meung's addition, formless and inconsistent
as it is, contributed as much or more to the poem's reputation as Guillaume's beginning. In both parts the ideal
of love is less intense, more bourgeois, than the feudal
aristocratic tradition of Provence from which it derives,
and in which the lady was worshipped almost as a god-

dess. But it was perhaps largely due to Jean that later poets felt there was nothing strange in using the device of a love-story to treat all kinds of philosophical and scientific matter in poetry. The habit of mind by which all subjects may be gathered in under the one heading of love is aptly summed up in the words of Thomas Middleton as late as 1623:

> Love has an intellect that runs through all
> The scrutinous sciences, and like a cunning poet
> Catches a quantity of every knowledge
> Yet brings all home into one mystery,
> Into one secret, that he proceeds in.

> *The Changeling*, Act III, Sc. 3

This seems precisely the medieval attitude. It is perhaps to Jean that we may attribute the awakening of those varied philosophical interests, and their poetic treatment, so notable in Chaucer. It may be that Chaucer's own *House of Fame* is an attempt to gather 'scrutinous sciences' into 'one mystery'.

There is also in Jean's addition both a bitter satire against women and an attempt to bring the law of love under God's guidance, to reconcile love and Reason. Again, the satire and the attempt to reconcile earthly love with the love of Reason are notable characteristics of Chaucer's poetry. He did not find these *motifs* in Jean alone, but there is every reason to guess that such interests were first fostered by the *Roman*. Indeed, the *Roman* gives us the scope of Chaucer's mind, his delight in young love, in science and philosophy, in rich description, in manners, in satire, in 'bold bawdry', all sheltered under the universal cloak of love and love's nobility, which does not refuse cover to some conflicting ideas. Nothing on earth need be alien to this kind of poetry.

It is, however, secular poetry, notwithstanding its Christian ideals and standpoint. It may be argued that Chaucer never completely assimilated directly religious poetry into his secular poetry, wide-embracing as that was. Chaucer tended to deal with his religion in terms of adapted pagan myth in order to adjust it to his secular inspiration. His excellent devotional verse stands a little apart in spirit from his other poetry. Only Dante seems to have been able to weld directly Christian love to other secular experience of love. So we must turn for the expression of Christian devotion in Chaucer to another early poem, *An A.B.C.* Like the *Roman* it is a translation from the French. It is very close in thought to the original, but already shows some freedom in the style, where Chaucer is more vivid and concrete in expression than the French poet. The poem is, however, a formal translation, fully in accord with the fourteenth century worship of the Blessed Virgin, and the commonplaces of medieval Christianity. Unoriginal and uninspired as it is, there is yet no reason to doubt its sincerity, its sense of sin, ardour of repentance, and desire for Heaven. Apart from some metrical interest, it is negligible as poetry, but it is important for reminding us that Chaucer's fundamental convictions were on the side of the Lady Reason, not of Cupid. It foreshadows the deep and tender piety which later informed Chaucer's devotional verse, and which was always present, if in the background of his mind. There was a force in this piety which would ultimately be satisfied only by Chaucer's own condemnation of all his great secular works.

Chapter Three

A WORKING COURTIER

LITTLE is known of Chaucer's other activities while he was writing these poems. He may have continued in Duke Lionel's retinue until 1367, though there is no evidence for this. But whatever he was doing, he must have remained in touch with the court; and judging from his later employments and poetry, he must have been adding to his knowledge of men and of books. The most interesting suggestion about his occupation in these ·unknown years is that he spent some time in one of the Inns of Court.[1] Where all is guesswork the slenderest clues are worth following up, though one must beware of giving them more importance than they actually possess, simply because they have no competitors. Professor Manly took up the comment of Thomas Speght, who in his edition of Chaucer in 1598 mentioned that 'Master Buckley did see a recorde in the same house (scil. the Inner Temple) where Geffrye Chaucer was fined two shillinges for beatinge a Franciscane Fryer in fletestreate'. Unfortunately these records no longer exist, but Master Buckley may well have been the official of that name whose duty it was to preserve the Temple records. And why should he invent? At least the legend is worth preserving for its own sake to save us from any conception of a merely gentle, whimsical Chaucer. The time was violent, and it was a common enough offence

[1] J. M. Manly, *New Light on Chaucer*, 1926.

32

among the young Templars. Men were far less restrained, a word was often enough followed by a blow (and a blow by death). As we *must* guess, it is a far better guess to think of Chaucer at this time (and perhaps later, too, in view of the awkward problem of his 'rape' of Cecily Chaumpaigne), as a man brimming with life and energy, a court gallant, passionate and sensitive; if not a Tybalt, at least a Romeo. We may guess he would have loathed the epithet 'gentle' in its modern sense as much as Charles Lamb did—'the meaning of gentle is equivocal at best, and almost always means poor-spirited'.

A legal education was likely enough for Chaucer. In the administration of the country men trained in law were beginning to compete with the clerics, and many of Chaucer's companions had had this training. A young man ambitious of distinction in civil life would find a desirable and usual education in one of the Inns of Court, for Oxford and Cambridge prepared a man only for holy orders. The account nearest to the Temple training of Chaucer's own day is given by Sir John Fortescue, whose own legal training began in 1414 in Lincoln's Inn. If a training similar to this was not actually Chaucer's, it was at least that of many men known to him. Students first entered an Inn of Chancery, about the age of sixteen. Here they studied the first principles of law, and after two years entered an Inn of Court. Fortescue writes:

Of these greater inns there are four in number, and some two hundred students belong in the aforementioned form to the least of them. In these greater inns, no student could be maintained on less expense than £13 6s. 8d. a year, and if he had servants to himself alone, as the majority have, then he will by so much the more bear expenses. Because of this costliness, there are not many who learn the laws in the inns except the sons of nobles. For poor and common people

cannot bear so much cost for the maintenance of their sons.
And merchants rarely desire to reduce their stock by such
annual burdens. Hence it comes about that there is scarcely
a man learned in the laws to be found in the realm, who is not
noble or sprung of noble lineage . . . In these greater inns,
indeed, and also in the lesser, there is, besides a school of
law, a kind of academy of all the manners that the nobles
learn. There they learn to sing and to exercise themselves
in every kind of harmonics. They are also taught there to
practise dancing and all games proper for nobles, as those
brought up in the king's household are accustomed to practise. In the vacations most of them apply themselves to the
study of legal science, and at festivals to the reading, after
the divine services, of Holy Scripture and of chronicles.
This is indeed a cultivation of virtues and a banishment of all
vice.[1]

This is an idealized account, but it shows at least what
was expected of an upper-class education. There is nothing in Chaucer's career or writings to conflict with such
a training, and a good deal to accord with it. Of course
his family were wine-merchants, but their connection
with the court may have made them ambitious for their
son, as is suggested by his position as page to the Countess
Elizabeth. And John Chaucer, as one of the leading
merchants in the City, was almost certainly wealthy
enough to give his son this expensive education. A legal
training would have been exceedingly valuable to Chaucer
in the many official positions he filled later in life.

Whatever the details, he was training for a court
career. The King's court itself, notwithstanding its
pageantry, was becoming more of an administrative
centre for the whole kingdom, unconsciously breaking
away from feudalism. A great historian of the fourteenth

---

[1] Sir John Fortescue, *De Laudibus Legum Anglie*, edited and translated by
S. B. Chrimes, Cambridge University Press, 1942, pp. 117–19.

century has summed up Chaucer's position in this development:

> There was an increasing tendency towards the building up of a homogeneous civil service within which circulation was unrestricted, and whereby a permanent career was more easily obtainable in the service of the state. Particularly noticeable was the tendency towards making the posts of the [royal] household the training ground of professional politicians. Even when dwelling in the king's court, these men were more than courtiers, and, on obtaining political charges, they showed that it was possible to combine their duty to the crown with general sympathy with the episcopal and baronial tradition of independent watchfulness of royal action. When the court officers did not rise to this higher level, they remained personally insignificant, and left little mark on history. Though anti-clericalism as a principle was no longer prominent, there remained a career for lay as well as for clerical talent. This was the inevitable result of the extension of education to circles outside the clerical sphere. There was the education of the court, which made the *miles literatus*, the knight who knew Latin, no longer a rare or an extraordinary phenomenon, as he had been in the reign of Henry III. How far a court training could under Edward III give a thorough culture to men, originating in the middle class of townsmen, and so remote from the clerical profession that the university had nothing to say to them, can well be illustrated by the career of that eminent civil servant, Geoffrey Chaucer. But a highly educated layman, like Chaucer, was still the exception in courtly circles. The real source of the destruction of the clerical monopoly of office was to be found in the excellent education which the law schools of London now gave to the common lawyers.[1]

Perhaps, as Professor Tout may not have realized, Chaucer was himself at least a partly trained lawyer.

[1] T. F. Tout, *Chapters in the Administrative History of Medieval England*, Vol. III, 1928, pp. 201–2.

Meanwhile, his father had died, his mother speedily re-
married, and he himself married. On 20 June 1367 he
was granted an annual salary of 20 marks (£13 6s. 8d.)
as a 'valectus' of the King's household. He was some-
where about twenty-five years old, just established
independently in life, his feet set on the lower rungs of
the ladder of advancement at the Court, which now takes
on the appearance not so much of a rose-garden as of the
social and administrative centre of the kingdom. The
language of this court, i.e. roughly the London dialect
of the South East Midlands, mixed with a variety of forms
from neighbouring dialects, such as those of Kent and
Middlesex, was at the beginning of its career as the
'King's English'. In 1363 Parliament was summoned
in English for the first time. This dialect has now been
slowly spread over all the country by social prestige, and
by the force of trade and civil administration. It is our
good luck (and lucky for Chaucer's fame) that he wrote
in this dialect, which has become the main form of modern English, rather than in any other regional dialect
which has been left stranded by the ebb of political,
economic and social history.

There can have been little home-life for the newly-
married Chaucers, for both were working courtiers.
Little is known about Philippa, and nothing personal.
She was probably the daughter of a knight of Hainault,
Sir Payne Roet, one of Queen Philippa's knights. She
was a 'domicella' or lady-in-waiting to the Queen, with
an annual salary of 10 marks (£6 13s. 4d.), and presumably a good match for Chaucer. The most interesting
thing about her is her connection by blood with a Court
scandal. For it was her younger sister Katharine, married to Sir Hugh Swynford, (d. 1372), who from 1371 or
1372 became the acknowledged mistress of John of

Gaunt. The scandal, however, lay not so much in this, as in their eventual marriage in 1396, when she became Gaunt's third wife. John of Gaunt's power in the kingdom was scarcely less than the king's, and his marriage to the daughter of a plain knight set the great ladies of the Court chattering with rage. They laid great blame on the Duke for marrying his concubine, says Froissart:

> for by reason thereof she shulde be the seconde person in honoure in Englande, whereby they sayd the quene shulde be shamefully accompanyed, and sayde, how surely they wolde nat come into no place where she shulde be presente; and moreover they sayde, it shulde be a great shame for theym, that suche a duchesse, come of so base a blode, and concubyne to the duke in his other wyfes dayes, shulde go and have the preemynence before them; they sayde their hertes shulde breke for sorrowe.

Op. cit., VI, p. 191.

This was not Chaucer's only connection with the greatest noble in the land, whom he may first have met at Hatfield when they were boys of roughly the same age. Chaucer's first considerable poem, *The Book of the Duchess*, was written on the death of Gaunt's first wife. Philippa Chaucer, moreover, when Queen Philippa died in 1369 became lady-in-waiting, like her sister Katharine, to Gaunt's second wife Constance, the Queen of Castile. Philippa besides her salary received various gifts from Gaunt, such as his New Year gifts in 1380, 1381, 1382, of a silver cup. She received her last payment on 18 June 1387 and probably died soon after this. Nothing is known of their family life. Probably Thomas Chaucer, who became wealthy and distinguished in the fifteenth century, was one of their sons. 'Little Lewis' for whom Chaucer wrote his *Treatise on the Astrolabe* was another, but has left no further trace. No other children are known. Philippa's gifts, and others that Chaucer received from Gaunt either jointly with her, or separately, are no evidence of special favour. They were simply part of the general system of remuneration, where wages were still partly in kind, in the form of food, drink, clothes and valuables.

From 1367 to 1369, therefore, both Chaucer and his wife were occupied in the Royal Household, with a modest but sufficient income. By 1368 Chaucer had become an Esquire of the King's Household. It was an age before personal service had come to be thought degrading, and his occupations varied between making beds and going on important ambassadorial messages. He remained an Esquire at least till 1378, perhaps later, and doubtless there was more bedmaking in the first year of his appointment than in the last. But it was not a job which the well-born despised. We get most of our information about it from Edward IV's Household Book (printed in the *Life-Records* by the Chaucer Society), which was based on earlier ordinances. There were four 'valecti' or 'Yeomen of Chambre', and they had to

> make beddis, to beare or hold torches, to sett boardis, to apparell all Chambers, and such othir seruices as the Chamberlaine, or Vshers of Chambre, comaunde or assigne; to attend the Chambre; to watche the King by course; to goe in messages, etc.

They were to eat in the King's chamber, or in the hall.

Of Squires of the Household there were to be forty, or more if the King so pleased, with the advice of his high counsel,

> chosen men in worship & of great worth: Also to be of sundry shires, to knowe the disposicion of the Cuntries; & of these, to be continually in Court, XX squiers attendantes

vppon the Kinges person, in Riding and going (i.e. walking),
& to serue his table from serveyeng bourd & other places, as
the Kinges Sewer will assigne them. Alsoe by assent amongst
them all, some to serue the Chamber at one tyme, some
the Hall at another tyme, of every messe that commeth from
the dressing bourd to their handes for such seruice, Soe
that thereof be nothing with-drawen by them, vppon such
paine as the Steward, Tresorer, comptroller, or the Judges
at the Comptingbourd in their absence, after their demerites,
will award; They eating in the Hall, sitting togither at both
meales after, as they serue, by assent. This was the old
manner, both for honour & profett of the King & his Court,
euery each of them taketh for his livery at night, dimidium
(i.e. a half) gallon ale; And for winter season, each of them
ij Candles parice, j faggot or els dimidium tallwood. And
when any of them is presente in Court, him is allowed for
wages daily in the Checkroll vijd ob. (i.e. sevenpence half-
penny); And clothing winter and sommer, of the Compting-
house, or els xls, it hath euer bine in speciall Charge to
squiers in this Court to weare the Coulour of the Kinges
liuery Customably, for the more glory, & in worshippinge
this honourable houshold.

The account goes on to regulate further details: They
shall keep one servant each, sleep two to a bed, pay for
the carriage of their bedding, not depart without leave,
keep no dogs in Court, etc. This is the tradition of
efficient organisation which occasionally drew down the
scorn of the captive French knights, but which nevertheless must have been enormously important in making
Edward III's Court so brilliant. And so here we find
Chaucer, expected to keep up a handsome appearance as
a personal servant and aide to the King, taking his part
in a well-run (for the times) administrative machine.
With twenty squires on duty and twenty off, his tasks
cannot have been heavy. The Household Book notes that:

D

These Esquires of housold of old be accustomed, winter and summer, in afternoones and in eueninges, to drawe to Lordes Chambres within Court, there to keep honest company after there Cunninge, in talking of Cronicles of Kinges, and of others Pollicies, or in pipeing or harpeing, synginges, or other actes marcealls, to helpe to occupie the Court, and accompanie estraingers, till the time require of departing.

We may imagine these gatherings, splendid as the frontispiece to a fifteenth-century copy of *Troilus*, in Corpus Christi College Library, Cambridge, when the great lords and ladies, as well as the less noble ranks, talked of Arms and Love, gossiped about the political news, heard songs and stories. Here the youthful Chaucer, in splendid livery, perhaps sang those lyrics, now lost, which caused Venus in Gower's poem to say:

> And gret[1] wel Chaucer when ye mete
> As mi disciple and mi poete:
> For in the floures of his youthe
> In sondri wise, as he well couthe,[2]
> Of Dities and of Songes Glade
> The whiche he for mi sake made,
> The lond fulfild is oueral.

At the end of his life, Chaucer asked for Christ's mercy for 'many a song and many a leccherous lay'. These splendid, sophisticated courtly gatherings were the primary audience Chaucer had in mind for his poems and even his sermons, for the *Miller's* or *Reeve's Tale* as well as the *Book of the Duchess* and the *Troilus*. The famous *Troilus* frontispiece shows Chaucer at the height of his fame in the late 'eighties reading to the assembled Court. Doubtless it is an idealized picture,[3] but it reminds us

---

[1] greet.   [2] knew.
[3] For an attempt at identification see Miss Margaret Galway's interesting article, *Modern Language Review*, Vol. XLIV, 1949, No. 2.

that Chaucer's is a courtly, aristocratic art. And apart from its own beauty it reminds us that poetry in Chaucer's time was still mainly heard, not read; and that reading aloud was the primary means of 'publishing' for Chaucer.

Though he must have attended many such gatherings and been known as one well fitted to 'occupy the Court', he had not reached in the 'sixties his later eminence as the supreme English poet. But he very soon achieved distinction with his first considerable poem that we know of, *The Book of the Duchess*, composed late in 1369 or early 1370. For our view of Chaucer's life it marks a moment of special interest. In one way it is a climax—the product of long and loving reading of Ovid, the *Roman*, Machaut, and Froissart, for it is a tissue spun almost entirely out of these. It shows more reading than this, but it is entirely conventional. It is a courtly poem written for John of Gaunt. So it sums up Chaucer's past development. On the other hand, the death of the Duchess Blanche whom it mourns, is like the first menacing roll of thunder from the storm which must shatter the Garden of the Rose. By implication we are directed towards a less enchanted world. There will be all the stress of a busy official life for Chaucer, but even more the cloudy spectacle of life and death as they always are. And perhaps the last half of the fourteenth century was grimmer than some, harried as it was by dreadful plague, drained by disastrous foreign war, with increasingly troubled civil government and misgovernment, culminating in Richard's deposition and murder. At the end of the decade we are just entering came the explosion of the Peasants' Revolt in 1381, which nearly overturned the Government, and was particularly hostile to John of Gaunt. In Chaucer's own artistic development, too, *The*

Book of the Duchess looks forward, for the poem is more than translation or imitation. Its vividness and pathos, its dramatic dialogue and strong construction are a delight in themselves and pledge of greater things to come. Above all, it already bears the genuine stamp of Chaucer's strong poetic personality.

The poem also points the contrast, ever present in Chaucer, between the background of important political and social events, and the subject-matter of his poetry. Chaucer never comments on the events of his own day. Yet they must have been much in his mind by the nature of his situation and occupation. They must have affected his ideas and temperament.

Although Chaucer does not mention it, the Duchess Blanche died of plague. The plague hung over the fourteenth century like a poisonous cloud, with few breaks, many showers, and now and again terrible storms. The worst storm was the Black Death of 1349, and the next worst was in 1369. Apart from the terror of such widespread death, the disease itself was so horrible. Hard lumps arose in the groin and armpit which were exceptionally painful and could not be lanced. Swellings, carbuncles, vomiting, spitting blood, were among the other symptoms. Sometimes the victims flung themselves out of their beds from pain and delirium. These were poor Blanche's sufferings. By 1380 between a third and a half of the population had perished so. In some places whole villages and tracts of land lay waste and uninhabited; but the towns suffered most with their crowded and insanitary conditions.

The fearful mortality hastened many changes which were bringing a new world with so many birth-pangs out of the old, but the immediate results were misery, derangement and loss. The progress of the arts and sciences was hindered where it was not stopped. The University of Oxford almost ceased to function for two or three years after the Black Death. The economic results were a great rise in prices and a great shortage of labour. Since special Statutes were enacted to keep wages down the strain on the poor became heavier, and the potential value of their labour quite disproportionate to its legal reward. Although it was a middle-class Parliament which tried to enforce the Statutes of Labourers, the great nobles who paid lip-service and more to the ideal of chivalry were the leaders of the country, and their government in this long crisis was bad. The Black Prince, the embodiment of fourteenth-century chivalry, has been characterized as 'great in tournaments, great in war, and master of a social code remarkable alike for senselessness, extravagance, and complete indifference to the interests of classes other than its own'.[1] We need not adopt such an extreme position of moral wisdom after the event to agree that the characteristically human selfishness, blindness and inflexibility of mind of all concerned were disastrous. The tournament of the rich was called the torment of the poor by the preachers who so unweariedly and wearisomely castigated the many vices of every class.

At the beginning of the thirteen-seventies there was much discontent at home fomented by impractically reactionary legislation. Abroad, the 'sixties had seen the last period of glory in the everlasting war. And just as at home continued mismanagement in the new decade culminated in the Peasants' Revolt, so abroad there was hitherto unparalleled disaster for England, when even the command of the Narrow Sea was lost, and the French raided and burnt English towns. This period began with

[1] A. Steel, *Richard II*, 1941, pp. 39-40.

a fruitless campaign starting in May 1369, which dragged
on for several years. The Black Prince, by an ill-advised
tax, stirred up trouble for himself in the English pro-
vince of Aquitaine, and stained his name with the merciless sack of Limoges. From 1369 Edward III, the last of
those 'champions of personal power, passionate and lustful men, who loved domination, strife, war, and the
chase'[1] who constituted the medieval kingly ideal, was
breaking up into a senile old man, dominated by his
avaricious mistress Alice Perrers.

What Chaucer thought of all this cannot be said. On
17 July 1368 he had gone to the Continent, while the
truce was still on, with a large sum of money on a mission
we know nothing about. Obviously he was by now in a
position of trust. When the war started again in 1369 he
was issued, with several others of the Esquires, with ten
pounds for his expenses in the French wars, but he seems
not to have been very long abroad, and perhaps went in
an administrative rather than in a fighting capacity. On
1 September he received an allowance, with Philippa his
wife, for mourning for Queen Philippa who died on 15
August. With her death 'the most brilliant court in
Europe became the most corrupt'.[2] The Duchess
Blanche died on 12 September. Chaucer presumably
composed his poem in the six months or so after this.
Gaunt returned to England in November and cherished
the memory of his charming young wife to the end of his
days. Chaucer may have returned with him, and perhaps
read his poem to the court in the early part of 1370.

The poem is derivative, ceremonial, and an elegy. Yet
the impression it leaves is of a direct sympathy, freshness,
and sweetness. It leaves a bright image in the reader's

---

[1] Ch. Petit Dutaillis, quoted A. Steel, *Richard II*.
[2] S. Armitage-Smith, *John of Gaunt*, 1904, p. 76.

mind of a beautiful, happy and serene girl, and of the happiness it was to know her. Nevertheless, the poem is a true elegy. It is not a private outcry of grief nor a private consolation. It seeks direction out by indirection, and even the Duchess Blanche is only obliquely referred to,

> And gode, faire, White, she hete.[1]
>
> l. 948

The poem is 'courteous' on every level from the social to the spiritual. The polite dialogue between the poet and the Black Knight (the grieving husband) shows the poet of an obviously lower rank, as we see from his use of the formal 'ye', 'yow', while the Black Knight addresses him as an inferior, 'thou', 'thee'. These good manners are also shown in the spiritual plane. The dream-setting, the beautiful formal description, allow no vulgar intrusion on a man (and a prince's) personal grief. The conventionality sets the situation at a distance, in bright, expected colours, like a medieval miniature. How else could we sympathize with one whom we loved and respected, much superior to us in rank, and not on terms of intimacy? The construction of the poem is very effective in the way it eases into the subject—first the poet's sleeplessness, and then the brief pathetic tale of Ceyx and Alcyone, where a wife mourns her dead husband—not told with passion, but deftly setting the elegiac tone of the whole piece. Chaucer takes the story from Ovid, but rightly leaves out the final metamorphosis of husband and wife into birds. Then the poet falls asleep, and describes how he dreamt he awoke on a delicious morning in a bright colourful room, and accompanied a great king's hunt, until he got lost in a mysterious forest, where he discovered the Black Knight mourning. It is the Knight's

[1] was called.

description of his lost love which is the eulogy of the Duchess Blanche. The description of her is diffuse and conventional; but the convention itself is still of power to interest and please us; the serene, sweet, golden-haired, beautiful lady; she is, after all, an archetypal image in our deepest consciousness; how should she fail to move us? Botticelli's Aphrodite, the wood of his Primavera, this is the lovely dream-world in which Chaucer summons up his story of bitter loss, and while the sense of loss remains, it is softened by the wonder and delight of what has been.

The poem is the work of an as yet immature poet. For all its assured good manners, its delicacy, its bright description, dramatic dialogue, breadth of reading, there is a lack of poetic control. Its derivativeness is nothing— lines from other men's poems must have floated in Chaucer's mind both consciously and unconsciously all his life long. Chaucer gives convention a neat turn to make it serve his purpose of elegy. But he is throughout too anxious to display his other reading, his medical knowledge, his historical knowledge, and so forth. This is a common fault of his time. Worse than this, he is laboriously diffuse and sometimes bathetic. But worst of all, he sometimes cannot control the tone he requires. When the messenger from Juno awakes Morpheus there is a brash heartiness about his call which is amusing enough in its way, but quite out of keeping with the poem. It is too alive and bright and colloquial. Whether Chaucer *intended* it to be amusing or not is difficult to say: but at least we can say it should *not* be amusing. Another instance of where he is perhaps too dramatic is in his dialogue with the Black Knight. The dullness of the poet is an excellent way of leading into the Black Knight's description because it makes question and reply seem quite natural. But it sometimes verges on the humorous —an effect which Chaucer quite certainly could *not* have intended, as can be seen from the circumstances and intention of the poem.

But notwithstanding its obvious faults, this is an excellent poem which turns an old convention to new use. Thus while the Black Knight's love-affair is rendered in the terms of the *Roman*, and there is almost a cento of quotations from the *Roman*, Froissart, and Machaut, the construction of the poem is Chaucer's own, and very good. Furthermore, the celebration of love is also the celebration of a love-marriage which there is no occasion to repent. There are many typical Chaucerian touches: freshness and firmness of description, humour, pathos, learning, and the capacity for rejoicing in human personality.

The Book of the Duchess does not provide any biographical material. The opening lines about the poet's own hopeless love are conventional and copied from a poem by Froissart. And even if the story of the Black Knight and his 'White' is true to the heart of Gaunt's love for Blanche, it is transposed into the conventional mode. Whatever Chaucer's private thoughts and feelings, poetry was not for him, nor for his age, a therapeutic device for easing himself of the pressure of his own emotions. *The Book of the Duchess* may be young man's poetry, but nothing could be further from youthful or egotistic self-expression. The poem is, however, one springing from personal relationships. There are no political or social interests displayed, for all its width of reference.

Chapter Four

DIPLOMAT AND CIVIL SERVANT

FROM 1370 to 1391 the mature Chaucer was busy on the King's occasions at home and abroad. He made a short trip overseas in the summer and autumn of 1370. Then on 1 December 1372 he left London on his first visit to Italy. He was one of three commissioners who were sent to negotiate a trade agreement with Genoa. Often one of such a group of commissioners was legally trained, and it may be that Chaucer owed his appointment to such a training. At any rate a special position of trust and responsibility seems to have been his, for he was detached on a secret mission to Florence, perhaps to negotiate a private loan for the King. He was back in London by 23 May 1373, so that allowing for travelling time, he spent two or three months in Italy, in winter and early spring. A few years later, in 1378, he spent July in Milan, on another diplomatic mission. His first visit in particular was of the greatest importance for the development of his poetry.

An Englishman visiting Italy today is usually entranced by its romantic beauty and enthralled by its richness in the visual arts. But he will not have to depend on a visit to the country for knowledge of its literature. Italy was something quite different for Chaucer. As to natural beauty, Chaucer like most men of his time had no eye for the picturesque. His favourite scenery was the tamed, controlled, pretty landscape of the *Roman*, or the charm of such a garden as he describes in the Prologue to *The Legend of Good Women*. Nature in the wild was too harsh and menacing and too near to be relished. As for the arts, Italy had already begun to show her greatness. Everywhere there were schools of painting and sculpture, and Giotto had already accomplished his life's work, though the supreme Italian artists had yet to arise. But the contrast cannot have been nearly so sharp to Chaucer as it is to us. For one thing, the highest peak of the artistic achievement of his time was in France, which he already knew. For another, England, though a small and provincial country compared with France, was itself not the least splendid in Europe. Indeed, the master-art, architecture, which alone had been carried on through the plague years, was perhaps richer in promise in England than in any other country. If Italy was rich in frescoes newly painted, so was England. English churches and great buildings did not rest soberly, as now, in the drabness of grey stone; they were richly decorated within and without. Westminster Abbey is said to have been whitewashed all over on the outside; the great West Front of Wells Cathedral, with all its statues, was painted in ochre. Within, tombs and shrines were painted, and plentifully adorned with statues plated with gold or silver, or with images of painted wood or stone. Enamels, ivories, jewels, abounded in the greater churches, whose walls were painted with great murals, parts of which may yet be seen in Winchester, Canterbury, Dorchester. The brilliance of the King's Chapel of Saint Stephen at Westminster must have rivalled that of any *sainte chapelle* in Europe. Even a humble village church would have its murals, sometimes as extensive and remarkable as those at South Leigh in Oxfordshire. Private houses on the larger scale had murals and pictured tapestries. The room the poet dreams he wakens in, as he tells in *The Book of the Duchess*, with painted walls and windows was surely not unique. As to easel pictures, there seems no reason to suppose the Wilton Diptych to be anything but a product of the court-art of Richard II, and it is one of the masterpieces of European painting of the time. Among the minor arts, a kind of embroidery was so famous as to be known simply as 'English work'—*opus Anglicanum*. Gold and silver work seems to have been plentiful and of a high standard. The style of all this splendour of the visual arts in fourteenth-century England was varied, vigorous, and independent. It was a worthy contribution to European culture, even if not so great as that of France, an altogether bigger and richer country. Since most of this art owed its inspiration to the doctrines of the Church (though a new worldly spirit has been detected in the latter part of the fourteenth-century) it was mostly destroyed by the Philistine fervour released by Henry VIII, and what little remained suffered sadly from the Puritans. But Chaucer at least need have felt no inferiority or surprise before the artistic achievements of the Continent.

Where he would have noticed London's almost rural backwardness was in commercial and industrial organization. Florence in particular was perhaps the chief industrial and financial city of Europe, holding a position comparable with London's in the early twentieth century. It was at least twice the size of the London of Chaucer. Florentines were the principal bankers of Europe (Edward III had borrowed very much money from them), and they had agents and correspondents everywhere. A relic of their importance in London still survives in the name Lombard Street. Florence was far ahead of London also in the production of books. For one thing, in the manufacture of paper, slowly beginning to supplement and eventually to supplant parchment, Italy had almost a monopoly. England had not one paper mill till 1490. And in Florence, Dante was venerated, and Petrarch and Boccaccio were still alive. A few months after Chaucer's first visit, Boccaccio was lecturing on Dante. In Italy certainly, and Florence probably, Chaucer first became acquainted with some of the Latin and Italian works of these great writers. It is probable that here too he laid the foundation of his own library—for Chaucer seems to have had an astonishing number of books for a private Englishman of his time. Even here, however, the limited currency of all books must have made his acquisitions to some extent casual and fortuitous. Manuscripts have no title-pages, and rarely tell the authors' names. Many miscellaneous items were bound up in one volume, and it was next to impossible to collect an author's works, because the author himself was largely ignored. One of the curiosities of literary history which illustrates these matters is Petrarch's total ignorance of the *Decameron* until a year or two before his death, although he and Boccaccio had been intimate for many years, and the *Decameron* a popular work. But Boccaccio in his later life was prouder of his Latin works, and even after Dante's great example, Latin had in general more prestige than the vernacular.

There is no evidence that Chaucer met Petrarch or Boccaccio and he remained in ignorance of the latter's very name, but he read some of their Latin and Italian works with the greatest eagerness. These and Dante he read and re-read, and the result was a continual enrichment and strengthening of his poetic powers throughout the rest of his life. It was not a case of the 'French influence' being changed for an 'Italian influence'. No new channel of development was created by his Italian reading; rather, fresh and more fertile waters poured down the earlier, shallower stream of his French manner, following the same direction, nourishing the same interests, but deepening and broadening the flow.

Chaucer learnt from the Italians new subjects, a new magnificence and control of diction, and a new ability to construct. The virtue of construction in a long poem is often absent from earlier medieval writers, partly because most poems were mainly intended to be heard, and oral delivery favours rambling and repetition. The prime virtues of good construction in a long poem, such as consistency, order, proper subordination of the less important to the more important, absence of rambling and repetitiveness, are rare in ages when there are very few readers. There is a library behind most great long poems, though with lyrics the case may be different. Florence was much in advance of London in the possession of books, and Chaucer far in advance of most of his fellow Englishmen. He was a mighty reader before the Lord, and perhaps one of very few who read 'as dumb as any stone'.[1] He is the first of a great book-collecting, book-reading class, that of the higher civil servant.

However, he took some time to digest his reading. The poem which most probably followed his Italian journey is the *Life of Saint Cecilia*, which was later put among the *Canterbury Tales* as the *Second Nun's Tale*, awaiting a revision it never received. The poem is a fairly close translation from Latin, in a style at once better and worse than that of his previous secular poems—less diffuse and pretentious, but also less rich, vivid and musical. It has a genuine warmth of devotion, the quiet

---

[1] H.F. ll. 656. Most people even when reading to themselves, used to read aloud. Cf. H. J. Chaytor, *From Script to Print*, 1945.

certitude of piety, an occasional pleasant freshness and prettiness of detail. The most striking things in it come in the Introduction, and Invocation to Mary. There is a clumsy first stanza about the wickedness of Idleness— the Devil finds work for idle hands to do. This is a conventional opening, and obviously aims at the *Roman* where the lovely portress of the Rose-garden is Idleness, but the arrangement of ideas seems to be Chaucer's own. He himself once translated part of the *Roman*; are we therefore to assume a change of heart? That is unlikely. It is simply a case of the predominance of one mood, or one artistic device, over the other. We must recognize Chaucer's capacity for, even his pleasure in, moving from one mood to its contradiction like a man moving from one room to another in the same house. There is in Chaucer's mind a profound duality, deriving ultimately from religious convictions, of which these pros and cons about Idleness are a superficial, though genuine, manifestation.

The other striking passage in the Introduction is the Invocation to the Blessed Virgin, a translation from Dante, where Dante's virtue shines through, clear, direct, elevated. It is an astonishing contrast in poetic merit to Chaucer's own unaided labourings with the common-place thought on idleness in the first stanza. The difference gives us some measure of the lesson the great Italian—greatest of all poets, some would say—was able to teach Chaucer. Henceforward there is something of Dante in nearly everything that Chaucer writes—a measure of the eagerness with which he learnt. Such a teacher, such a learner: the Italian poet who sums up in himself the power, universality, passion and beauty of the Middle Ages; the English poet in the making, a ripe man, devout, yet rich in worldly experience of court and

business, love and taxes, interested in so much, understanding so much. But as we see from these two passages,
placed so near, yet so far apart in merit, Dante's influence needed time to be absorbed.

Another witness to Chaucer's struggle to assimilate
the Italian manner is *Anelida and Arcite*. Although what
there is of the conventional plot seems to be of Chaucer's
own devising, the poem is one (and perhaps the first) of
several to make use of Boccaccio's *Teseide*. It is presumably to be dated not too long after his return from
Italy. The theme of a deserted lady is one that was dear
to Chaucer for many years. The poem begins with an
attempt at epic magnificence in the Italian style, but
suddenly dwindles to a *Complaint* by Anelida, which
shows great metrical skill, but is otherwise thin and
conventional in the French manner. Though skilful in
itself, it ruins the general structure, and Chaucer abandoned the poem.

Chaucer returned from Italy in May 1373, and probably his wife had to go almost immediately to Tutbury
Castle in Staffordshire with Gaunt's second wife, Queen
Constance of Castile, to whom she was lady-in-waiting.
Since Chaucer personally received payments at Westminster in the following November and February, they
were presumably separated a good deal. If they were a
devoted couple they were unlucky, though many other
esquires and ladies-in-waiting were in a similar position.

In the spring things improved rapidly. On 23 April
1374, during the Garter feast of St. George, Chaucer was
granted a pitcher of wine daily (later commuted to an
annual grant of 20 marks—£13 6s. 8d., a fair sum). A
fortnight later (10 May 1374) he obtained the dwelling-
house above the city gate of Aldgate, for no rent, though
he had to keep it in repair. Such a dwelling was pleasant

and convenient and Chaucer was lucky to get it. It must have been obtained by influence with the City, though we do not know whose. The house was obviously taken to prepare for his new appointment, which came four weeks later. On 8 June 1374, Chaucer was appointed Comptroller of the Customs and Subsidy of wools, skins, and tanned hides in the Port of London, with the usual fees. His place of business was about ten minutes' walk from his new house. Five days later (13 June) he and his wife received an annuity of £10 for life from Gaunt, which was presumably a recognition of Philippa's services now that she was leaving to set up house for the first time. From the fact that Gaunt returned to London at the end of April, some have seen his hand in these advancements of Chaucer's. It has even been inferred that Philippa was one of Gaunt's several cast-off mistresses. But there is no evidence for this. Gaunt had come back to great unpopularity from his disastrous French expedition; he would not have been likely to have had influence with the City, and might well have rewarded Philippa generously for legitimate services, especially as her sister had been his mistress for two or three years.

Chaucer's new appointment was not a sinecure. He was to write out the rolls of his office with his own hand, and perform his duties personally. These were mainly to act as check on the two collectors, who were such men of substance as Nicholas Brembre, William Walworth (the Lord Mayor who murdered Wat Tyler), and John Philipot. These were important businessmen in the City. Chaucer's income was £10 a year, probably a good deal increased by fees, and once at least, by £71 4s. 6d., being the fine of a merchant whom Chaucer detected shipping wool without paying duty. The house at Aldgate and his work at the Customs were Chaucer's main concerns until 1385 or 1386. While here at least two sons, Lewis and Thomas, were born, and he composed *The House of Fame*, *The Parliament of Fowls*, *Troilus and Criseyde*, and several minor poems, besides translating Boethius' *Consolation of Philosophy*. He may have thought of *The Canterbury Tales* here, and even written some of them. It is an astonishingly productive period. There is an amusing and interesting passage in the *House of Fame* referring to this time where he represents himself as being reproached (by an Eagle) for his dullness, of all things, because being chained to the office desk all day and reading half the night he sees nothing of his very neighbours. Perhaps there is an underlying suggestion here (not necessarily conscious) both of his impatience at his office drudgery, and his escape from it into imaginative flights of the mind, as symbolised by his flight with the Eagle. Jupiter has considered, the Eagle says, how dutifully Chaucer has laboured in writing songs of love, without any reward, and also,

> beau sir, other thynges;
>
> That is, that thou hast no tydynges
> Of Loves folk, yf they be glade,
> Ne of noght elles that God made;
> And noght oonly fro fer contree
> That ther no tydynge cometh to thee,
> But of thy verray neyghebores,
> That duellen[1] almost at thy dores,
> Thou herist neyther that ne this;
> For when thy labour doon al ys,
> And hast mad alle thy rekenynges,
> In stede of reste and newe thynges,
> Thou goost hom to thy hous anoon,
> And also domb as any stoon,

[1] dwell.

Thou sittest at another book
Tyl fully daswed[1] ys thy look,
And lyvest thus as an heremyte,
Although thyn abstynence ys lyte.[2]
  And therfore Joves, thorgh hys grace,
Wol that I bere the[3] to a place
Which that hight[4] the Hous of Fame,
To do the[3] som disport and game.

H.F. 643–664

However, Chaucer's occupations were not continu-
ously sedentary. He was sent abroad several times on
commissions handling delicate negotiations to stop the
war with France, and trying to arrange the marriage of
the ten-year-old Prince Richard with Marie of France.[5]
(Neither object was achieved.) There is every reason to
suppose him high in favour at court, and regarded as an
accomplished courtier, diplomat and administrator.

On 26 June, 1377, Edward III, for some years in
his dotage, at last died, and the child Richard acceded to
the throne. All Chaucer's posts and emoluments were
formally renewed, and in January 1378 he was again
abroad negotiating on the same delicate matters. From
28 May to 19 September, 1378 he was again in Italy,
in Milan, negotiating with Bernabo Visconti, and the
famous English *condottiere*, Sir John Hawkwood. During
this latter absence he granted the poet John Gower
powers of attorney to act for him, so they were evidently
good friends. This was the last time Chaucer went
abroad on the king's business.

---

[1] dazed.   [2] little.   [3] thee.   [4] was called.
[5] Thus in December 1376 he was associated with Sir John Burley, Captain
of Calais, on a secret mission: from February to March 1377, he went on a
mission to Paris, Montreuil and elsewhere, with Sir Thomas Percy (later Earl
of Worcester). He was away again April 30th to June 26th, 1377. He seems
to have been associated with Sir Guiscard d'Angle (one of Richard's tutors) and
Sir Richard Stury, in the marriage negotiations.

It was a period of continuing prosperity for him. He and his wife received a steady flow of payments and gifts. There was the fine, mentioned earlier, and in November and December 1378 he was granted two lucrative wardships. However the smooth progress was marred by two incidents, one private, one public. The first is suggested by the deed, dated 1 May 1380, whereby one Cecily Chaumpaigne released Geoffrey Chaucer Esquire of every sort of action 'both of my rape (meo raptu), and of any other matter or cause'. On the face of a release it might seem that Chaucer was not guilty, but many critics have held that there is no smoke without fire. *Raptus* may mean abduction of the kind of which Chaucer's father was the victim, or it may mean rape in the modern sense. Chaucer may have been guilty of either or both, though the latter seems unimaginable. All we can say is that whatever tangled story lies behind this curious document it impeded neither Chaucer's career nor the regard of his friends. The names of witnesses and friends of Chaucer appearing in the document are those of distinguished men: Sir William Beauchamp, Chamberlain of the King, and for long one of Chaucer's circle; John de Clanvowe and William de Nevylle, two of those serious-minded 'Lollard Knights'; John Philipot, grocer, Collector of Customs, and later a Lord Mayor of London. These were all men of the 'King's party' at Court (as were the lawyer Strode, and Gower, to whom the *Troilus* is dedicated) and with the two latter give an excellent cross-section of the friends who made up Chaucer's more intimate circle of acquaintances—solid men, courtiers, merchants, men of learning, all closely associated.

The other incident which must have disturbed Chaucer was a disaster of national dimensions—the Peasants' Revolt, when in June 1381 a wild mob stormed the city, and for three days held it under a reign of terror, the objects of their particular hostility being lawyers, collectors of the King's taxes, John of Gaunt and his followers, and the wretched immigrant Flemish weavers. There was some incendiarism and Gaunt's splendid house, the Savoy, in the Strand, was totally destroyed. There were many killings; the aged and gentle Archbishop Sudbury, regarded as the representative of oppressive Government, being Chancellor, was haled out of the Tower and beheaded; and many Flemish weavers suffered. The rebels were, however, pathetically loyal to the person of the King, and the Revolt was calmed down, as is well known, by Richard's bold meeting with the peasants. He made a promise of general pardon, which was followed a few weeks later by the punishment of all those in any way implicated. Chaucer's friend Gower (a small landowner in Kent) represents the characteristic and understandable view of the upper classes when in his poem *Vox Clamantis* he represents the peasants as domestic beasts gone suddenly and outrageously mad.

Chaucer kept his views to himself; he was not a man fanatically to espouse one party or another. The orthodoxy, the idealism, the conviction of the world's sinfulness which are the ground-bass of his poetry, lead us to expect nothing else. His summing-up of experience which is the nearest thing we have to a personal expression of emotion about the world may well have been written within a few years of these events. It is to be found in the Balades, *Gentilesse* and *Lak of Stedfastnesse*. *Lak of Stedfastnesse* is the poem of a man who must equally condemn both the Revolt and the cruel and teacherous means of quelling it:

> Trouthe is put doun, resoun is holden fable;
> Vertu hath now no dominacioun;

> Pitee exyled, no man is merciable;
> Through covetyse is blent[1] discrecioun.[2]
> The world hath mad a permutacioun
> Fro right to wrong, fro trouthe to fikelnesse,
> That al is lost for lak of stedfastnesse.

Wickedness and misery are seen as springing from 'instability', i.e. from lack of loyalty, and the consequent upsetting of the proper order of society. The *envoy* to King Richard in the same poem aligns Chaucer with the usual political theories of his day, in both their punitive and idealistic forms:

> O prince, desyre to be honourable,
> Cherish thy folk and hate extorcioun!
> Suffre nothing that may be represable
> To thyn estat don in thy regioun.
> Shew forth thy swerd of castigacioun,
> Dred God, do law, love trouthe and worthinesse,
> And wed thy folk agein to stedfastnesse.

But behind and beneath this is the even more fundamental Christian and Boethian combination of resignation to fortune, and contempt of the world. Such an attitude is most clearly found in *Truth*, written when Chaucer was a good deal older. At this earlier and most successful period of his life Chaucer was less inclined to deny the world: nevertheless the doctrine of rejection was at all times an important element in his thought, and it may well be mentioned in connection with this crisis: ('trouthe' here means also God):

> That thee is sent, receyve in buxumnesse[3]
> The wrastling[4] for this world axeth[5] a fal.
> Her is non hoom, her nis but wildernesse:

[1] blinded.   [2] true perception.
[3] obedience.   [4] wrestling.   [5] asks.

Forth, pilgrim, forth! Forth, beste, out of thy stal!
Know thy contree, look up, thank God of al;
Hold the heye[1] wey, and lat thy gost thee lede;
And trouthe thee shal delivere, it is no drede[2].

Chaucer continued at the Customs House until 1386, apparently with all success. In November 1381 he received ten marks as a reward for diligence, and in 1382 he was appointed controller of the petty customs in the port of London. This latter was also probably a reward, as he was allowed to appoint a permanent deputy. In February 1385 he applied to exercise his main controllership also by permanent deputy. As in each of the two preceding years he was allowed to be away from his post for a month or so to attend to his private affairs, it seems he was breaking away from his administrative duties. He was appointed a Justice of the Peace for Kent in October 1385, and in August 1386 became Knight of the Shire to attend the Parliament of October, and it is usually thought that he went to live in Kent some time in 1385. His house over Aldgate was leased to another man in October 1386, and in December his two controllerships were granted to two other men. It is possible that he voluntarily resigned, but more likely that he lost them, though not for inefficiency. The reason is more probably to be found in the tangle of Court politics. There were three main factions, a 'court' or 'King's party', of whom, according to Mr. Steel, Sir Simon Burley was the leader; a Lancastrian faction, grouped round John of Gaunt; and a baronial opposition led by the Dukes of Gloucester and Warwick, and some others, which hated the Lancastrians and was largely contemptuous of the court. In 1386 the barons struck first at the Lancastrians, who were in uneasy alliance with the court party, and then, even more

[1] high.   [2] doubt.

devastatingly, at the court party. The barons succeeded, temporarily, in 'capturing' the King's authority and the royal administration. Chaucer seems to have been associated principally with the court-party, as were most of his circle. There was a purge of the king's men from administrative posts, and Mr. Steel considers this to be the reason for Chaucer's loss of his controllerships. It was an uneasy and dangerous time, and Chaucer may have felt himself well out of it down in Kent.

Chapter Five

THE INTELLECTUAL BACKGROUND: BOETHIUS
AND VENUS

THE years of business at the Customs-house were also
extraordinarily full of literary activity, both reading
and writing. Chaucer's intellectual interests led him to
delight in knowledge for its own sake, and for the sake of
understanding the full spectacle of life. In this period he
translated the great work of Boethius, *The Consolation of
Philosophy*. His interest in astronomy and astrology (the
two were indistinguishable in his day) now appears as an
important element in his thought. His interest in the
psychology of dreams and in physics is shown in *The
House of Fame*. The many references to the natural
sciences and to medicine in *The Canterbury Tales* doubtless reflect reading of which at least part was done at this
period. None of these many subjects can be considered
as diverging from, or hostile to, his poetry. They were
in part the very material of his poetry; and they helped
to focus his view of the world, of human character, of the
course of good and ill in human life. The desire for a
total view, a *Summa*, of earthly knowledge and experience, is a characteristic of the men of the High and Late
Middle Ages, whether they wrote in prose or verse.
There are such encyclopaedists as Vincent of Beauvais and
the Englishmen Alexander Neckham and Bartholomew;
the great theologians, St. Albertus Magnus and St.
Thomas Aquinas; and chief among poets, Dante. Chau-

cer's contemporary Langland and his friend Gower each attempted similar syntheses, and *The Canterbury Tales* are partly to be understood in this light. *The House of Fame* and the *Parliament* are also probably attempts at synthesis, for when a learned and courtly poet wished to gather in the whole created universe, he bound it together with 'the fayre chain of love'.

Some understanding, therefore, of the bases of Chaucer's thought about the world is necessary for understanding his poetry. The two main props of the structure of his thought are the Boethian philosophy; and astrology, which far from being charlatanry was the master-science of the times.

The precise date of his translation of Boethius's *Consolation of Philosophy* is uncertain. It was probably done some time about 1380, although it is likely he knew the book some years before that, while much of its substance was treated in the *Roman*. The translation was written with scholarly care, and at least two commentaries seem to have been consulted. Indeed, Chaucer was so intent on rendering his author's exact meaning that at times he is so anxiously literal as to be almost incomprehensible, But although his version is occasionally awkward and crabbed, most of it is clear, and some of it is excellent.

The subject-matter of the *Consolation* may be summed up in Milton's description of the Fallen Angels, who reasoned high

> Of Providence, Foreknowledge, Will and Fate—
> Fixed fate, free will, foreknowledge absolute—
> And found no end, in wandering mazes lost.
> Of good and evil much they argued then,
> Of happiness and final misery,
> Passion and apathy, and glory and shame—

though Boethius did not lose himself in the labyrinth.

Modern technical philosophy seems to some extent to have discarded these problems, but they must concern any man who thinks deeply. Boethius's first and undisputed premise is belief in a good and all-powerful God, who can do no evil, and who has created the world. This granted, he is obviously faced with two great difficulties. First, how can a good God have allowed so much misery and evil to enter the world? Secondly, since such a God must know *everything*, He knows the future. If God knows now what is going to happen in the future, then the future must be fixed, and nothing we can do can alter it. (This connects with the first problem, since it ultimately implies that God makes us do evil as well as good, whether we will or no.) The horror of this predestination, this determinism, appals Boethius, and he spends much time confuting it. Indeed, a great deal of the philosophy of the Middle Ages was concerned with it, and the philosophical poets, Dante and Jean de Meung, write about it. It is one of the dominant themes of learned controversy in England in the fourteenth century, and Chaucer often refers to it.

Boethius solves the problem of pain and evil by saying that although we all rightly and naturally desire happiness, we seek it under the wrong forms (as in the love of wife and family, of wealth and power, of natural scenery, of the arts). True happiness is the Good, which is God Who only is permanence. We should therefore love God alone; and to do this we must master ourselves and our natural passions. If we master our passions, we shall be free from the trammels of the world, and so shall find true happiness and freedom in God.

He solves the problem of predestination by first pointing out that eternity is quite different from time-going-on-for-ever. It is outside time (Boethius would have been

quite at ease with the modern physicist's definition of
time as the fourth dimension). Everything on earth, past,
present and future, is in God's eternal Now. Secondly,
he says that it is a man's passions only which are part of
the normal chain of inevitable cause and effect. Once his
soul has freed itself from the domination of the passions
by loving the divine, man's will is free.

This bleak summary of the central thought of the *Consolation* conveys nothing of its delight—the noble conception of an all-wise, loving Creator, of the loveliness of
the world as created by God, and as continually maintained by Him. There is an inevitable dualism in the
Consolation which is of extreme importance in appre-
ciating both Chaucer's thought, and that of the Middle
Ages as a whole. God is good, and therefore His creation
must be good: yet we know that so much is bad. Should
we, therefore, in loving God, despise His world? It seems
wrong to undervalue the world, since God made it 'and
saw that it was good', but if we love the world, do we
not inevitably forget God, loving His gifts instead of Him?

Most thinkers in the Middle Ages tended to emphasize
the need to be on the safe side, and to despise mundane
affairs. Chaucer himself translated Pope Innocent III's
De Contemptu Mundi (though the translation is lost) and at
the end of his life condemned his own mundane writings.
The dualism of medieval Christian teaching could provide an agonizing problem for an intelligent, sensuous
and pious man—especially in matters of love. However,
at this full flowering period of his life, Chaucer was most
attracted by the possibility of synthesis. Probably the
writers of the twelfth-century School of Chartres showed
him the way, but the possibility of reconciliation is inherent in the *Consolation* itself, as may be seen from
two important passages which Chaucer later put into

poems. One is in praise of God's creative activity; Boethius says that the world is *perfectly made*, and is governed and controlled by God's everlasting Reason, which binds the elements in harmony.[1] The other passage praises the harmony and stability of the creation, and says that 'this accordance of things is bound with Love, that governs earth and sea and has also command of heaven'. Love not only controls the physical universe but also 'holds together people joined with a holy bond, and knits (the) sacrament of marriages of chaste loves'.[2]

These and similar passages emphasize the goodness of creation and the divine source of love. Human love and marriage appear as part of the divinely maintained order of things. Love and reason here spring from the same source. The possibility of reconciling the inherent tension between them was further improved by the teachings of astrology.

One of the constant notes of the *Consolation* which must have especially appealed to Chaucer, is the praise of the beauty of the starry heavens which are the perfect example of the beauty of the natural world when it obeys God's laws. They are the embodiment of the serenity and radiance and perfect order—those brave translunary things—which are so notably lacking in our sphere beneath the moon. But all men in the fourteenth century believed in the influence of the stars, especially of the seven planets, either singly or in relation to each other and the signs of the Zodiac. The more learned the scientist or theologian (they were often combined in the same person) the more firmly he believed that the weather, the crops, the very stones of the earth, and all animal life including the animal part of human beings,

[1] *Consolation*, III, metre 9, repeated in Theseus's speech, *Knight's Tale*, *Canterbury Tales*, I (A), 2987 ff.

[2] *Consolation*, II, metre 8, repeated in Troilus's song, *Troilus*, III, 1743 ff.

were governed in their properties by the stars. The theory of astrological influences was the fourteenth-century scientific theory of the normal working of cause and effect now explained in terms of Newton's and Einstein's laws of dynamics and so forth. Medical men, scientists, politicians, merchants would have been incompetent if they did not either know some astrology or (in the two latter classes) consult the experts. The troubled and harassed years of the fourteenth century, especially after the Black Death, gave a great impetus to men's desire to know the future, and so perhaps to be able to control their fates. But, of course, the possibility of knowing the future immediately raised the problems of predestination faced by Boethius, while orthodox Christian doctrine was irrevocably committed to belief in free-will. Furthermore, the aim of controlling man's outer environment, rather than his inner spiritual state, is one which any religion must regard with misgiving. Hence there was a good deal of religious writing against science, in particular against astrology, not so much because it was thought to be untrue, as because it was thought that it might lead men on the wrong track. Those parts of the science which tended to destroy belief in freedom of the will (judicial astrology) or which appeared to truckle with supernatural (and probably evil) agents were especially condemned as magic. Professor Thorndyke has amply proved that science and magic spring from the same impulse of the mind to control the external rather than the internal world, and it often seems that what men call magic is rather faulty science. Astrology, to fourteenth-century minds, merged imperceptibly into magic, but it was difficult to draw the dividing line. This explains the many contradictions and confusions in writers on the subject, and Chaucer's own *volte-face* in the

Astrolabe (II. 4), where after he has gone on from astronomical information to the discussion of fortunate and
unfortunate aspects of the stars, he suddenly says,
'Natheles these ben observaunces of judicial matere and
rytes of payens, in whiche my spirit hath no feith'. The
crux of the problem lay, of course, in questions of morals
and ethics. Philosophical and religious problems were
not so obvious in the case of, say, weather-predictions.
The orthodox view with regard to men's actions may be
summed up in the words of St. Thomas Aquinas:

> The majority of men, in fact, are governed by their passions,
> which are dependent on bodily appetites; in these the in-
> fluence of the stars is clearly felt. Few indeed are the wise who
> are capable of resisting their animal instincts. Astrologers,
> consequently, are able to foretell the truth in the majority
> of cases, especially when they undertake general predictions.
> In particular predictions they do not attain certainty, for noth-
> ing prevents a man from resisting the dictates of his lower
> faculties. Wherefore the astrologers themselves are wont
> to say 'that the wise man rules the stars', forasmuch, namely,
> as he rules his own passions.[1]

Chaucer, it may be noted, does not make his heroes 'wise
men'.

The stars, therefore, are thought to form and often to
motivate a person's character. In Chaucer's work at this
period there is little emphasis on *resisting* the course
guided by the stars. The reason is that God's Providence
—or as he puts it in the *Knight's Tale*,

> The destinee, ministre general
> That executeth in the world over al
> The purveiaunce that God hath seyn biforn—
> > *Canterbury Tales*, I (A), 1663–5

[1] *Summa Theologica*, 1.1.115.4. Ad Tertium (5.544). Quoted by T. O.
Wedel, 'The Medieval Attitude toward Astrology', *Yale Studies in English*,
LX, Yale, 1920.

which controls the whole world with the 'chain of love', must intend all for the best. There is a strong streak of optimistic determinism in Chaucer's thought at this time. Since Love is what guides the world and maintains its order, as both Boethius and the Gospel of St. John say, the planet of love—Venus—assumes particular importance. Venus the planet was regarded as the scientific or immediate 'cause' of love not only between human beings, but of the 'love' which guides the mating of animals, and even the attraction asserted by the force of gravity (for to the fourteenth century the whole material universe was in a sense 'alive', almost sentient). Moreover, Venus was the Goddess of Love in much of the classical literature which Chaucer knew so well— stories of her marriage to Vulcan, and of her adultery with Mars, of her son Cupid, her son Aeneas, and of many an amour were well known to him and to many late-medieval writers. So many writers had told and retold these stories by Chaucer's time that there was an extraordinary confusion of tales and opinions, only added to by the various names attributed to her. The problem was to sort out the basis of scientific fact from the fictions of poets. There were many mythographers who attempted this from the fourth century onwards. The best of these was Boccaccio, who compiled the *De Genealogia Deorum*, a compendium which gathers up all its predecessors, often copying them literally. Chaucer may have known it, but anyway it shows the kind of knowledge he had. Boccaccio gives the scientific effects of all the planets, and relates, with analyses, many of the stories connected with their names. Venus is the most important, and will serve as example for the rest.

Boccaccio is not quite clear how many Venuses there are, but it is vital to realise that there are more than one.

The first is the Greater Venus, sixth daughter of the Sky and the Day. Boccaccio comments on the many confused stories about her, but as they have been deduced from the properties of the Planet, he says, he will first describe what the Astrologers say. The core of the matter is this. Since as a planet she appears fixed in the sky and moving with it, she seems to be produced by it, hence her father is the Sky. She is called daughter of the Day because of her brightness. Since God made nothing in vain, he made the stars 'in order that by their movement and influence, the seasons of the passing year should be varied, mortal things generated, what generated should be born, what born fostered, and in time should come to an end'. The effects of Venus are those of 'love, friendship, affection, company, domesticity, union between animals, and especially the begetting of children. . . . Whence it may be admitted that by her are caused the pleasures of men.' When she attends marriages she wears the girdle called the Ceston, signifying love, friendship, eloquence and caresses. 'This bond is not carried if not in honest marriage, and therefore all other coupling is called incest.' At times the astrologers say she is associated with the Furies, and this is especially liable to happen in spring, when 'not only brute animals, but also women, whose complexion is for the most part warm and moist when spring comes, incline more strongly towards heat and wantonness. Which inclination, if modesty does not restrain it, may be converted into fury.' The Furies may also be said to come when there is bitterness or deceit or desertion in love. Venus can also indicate mere sexuality, and the lustful are born under her domination.

The second Venus is the seventh daughter of the Sky, and mother of Cupid. By her Boccaccio understands the *lascivious* life, as referred to above. She signifies sexual intercourse. 'They paint Venus floating, to show that the life of unhappy lovers is joined with bitterness, and fought against by various fortunes with frequent shipwrecks. . . . They give roses into her care, because they redden and sting, which is appropriate to wantonness, insomuch as from the brutishness of the crime we become red, and by the consciousness of the sin we are pricked by a sting. And also, as the Rose delights us for a certain space, and shortly withers, wantonness also is a brief joy, and a cause of long penitence.' Cupid is her son. (This should be compared with Chaucer's description, *House of Fame*, 130 ff. The doves also signify wantonness, according to Boccaccio or rather, to Fulgentius, whom Boccaccio is transcribing here.)

The third Venus, eleventh daughter of Jove, was wife of Vulcan, mistress of Mars, mother of Aeneas. Some think she was the same as that lady of Cyprus who was wife of Adonis. But Boccaccio thinks not. It was this latter lady who invented prostitution in order to cover her own promiscuity.

Boccaccio does not, of course, believe in the pagan gods, any more than does Chaucer. Both confuse us (and perhaps themselves) by considering the stories as moral lessons and as exemplifying the wide variety of attributes of the planet. Furthermore, in their poems they were less worried about certain kinds of consistency than we are now. Venus, under various guises, appears in all the poems of this period, *The House of Fame*, *Parliament of Fowls*, *The Knight's Tale*, and *Troilus and Criseyde*.

Chapter Six

A PHILOSOPHICAL POET

*T*he House of Fame, like the *Anelida*, is unfinished. It may be another casualty to the new standard of form which Chaucer found in his Italian reading. *The House of Fame* is not in fact formless, but it proceeds somewhat crabwise after the fashion of the *Roman*, whereas Chaucer had seen in Dante and Boccaccio the possibilities of a more artistic structure. *The House of Fame* also reminds one of the *Roman* by its octosyllabic metre and by the discursive treatment of scientific and other matters within the framework of a love-vision. The sleeplessness, the dream, the discussion of dreams, the precise date, the guide, are all common properties of French love-visions. Yet there are strikingly new things, too. For example, the Temple of Venus which, under various significances, occurs here, in the *Parliament*, and in the *Knight's Tale*, is a new ingredient in such poems. The picture of Fame, though owing something to Virgil and Boethius and to the current images of Love and Fortune, is very unusual, as is the House of Twigs. It is surprising that the guide should be an eagle. There is therefore no lack of originality of invention. More than this, there is a new delight in the poem, a slightly mocking humour playing like dappled light and shade over the surface of a stream, brightening and diversifying the general flow and purpose without hurrying or impeding it. But even the humour

comes and goes, and the poem stops abruptly just before
some important announcement is to be made.

The First Book opens lightheartedly, but the main
story is of Chaucer's dream of the Temple of Venus,
which is all made of glass, and where he sees a picture of
Venus 'naked floating in a sea' with her rose garland,
comb and doves, and accompanied by Cupid and Vulcan.
This is sufficient, in the light of what the mythographers
say, to suggest that it is the lascivious Venus and painful
betrayed love, of which this is the temple. And so it
proves, for on the walls is written the story of the *Aeneid*,
which Chaucer proceeds to tell from the point of view of
the Middle Ages, as the story of the seduction and
betrayal of Dido by Aeneas, Venus's son. It is related
with the thin pathos which Chaucer had always at command for such stories, and it is amplified somewhat
frigidly with references to other ladies of classical antiquity, faithful but betrayed, whose stories seem to have
affected him all his life.

The proem of the Second Book returns to the sportive
tone of the Introduction to the First. Chaucer makes a
playfully exaggerated claim for the outstanding worth of
his dream, and comprehensively invokes Cipris, the
Muses, and his own Thought. (He seems to call Venus
Cipris only when he is thinking of her as the wanton
Venus, mistress of Mars.) The story of the dream is then
lightheartedly continued. The poet dreams he is swept
up into the heavens by an eagle. He is stunned with fear
and astonishment, for which the Eagle admonishes him
pretty sharply, softening enough, however, to explain to
him that Jupiter has taken pity on him because he has
served blind Cupid and fair Venus so 'ententyfly', 'with-
oute guerdon ever yit'—in other words, because he has
had no illicit love affairs. Then follows the famous pass-

age describing Chaucer's writings on love, how he studies far into the night because he must work during the day, and so knows nothing of how the world goes. As a reward he is to be taken to the House of Fame, where he will find news of love and all the variety of love's experience. Chaucer refuses to believe that this is possible; whence follows the Eagle's celebrated lecture on the properties of sound, which is excellent poetry at a not very exalted level. It finishes with the Eagle's amusing crow of self-satisfied triumph, after which he shows the poet the heavens, 'gladding' him with his explanations. It is characteristic of Chaucer that as he looks about and sees the 'airish beasts' and the way the clouds, rains and winds are made, he breaks out

> 'O God', quod y, 'that made Adam
> Moche ys thy myght and thy noblesse.'

> H.F. 970–1

It is equally characteristic that when the Eagle is anxious to inform him about the names of the stars, the poet says he is too old to learn. The Eagle points out how useful such knowledge will be 'when thou redest poetrie', but Chaucer says he will rely on the writer's words, and that anyway he is so near the stars that they will blind him if he looks at them. Then he is landed at Fame's 'place'.

This second book is entirely successful and delightful. The enthusiastic learned and talkative Eagle is the same kind of humorous character as Scott's Antiquary or Baron Bradwardine, save that his knowledge is, for his times, more up to date. We both smile at him and respect him. The apprehensive poet, with his terse replies, makes a perfect foil. Their dialogue is natural and amusing, and the metre smooth and varied. The material of the book, at first sight irrelevant, is in fact not so. There

is a piquant humour in having a suitably scientific reason
for the fantasy of the House of Fame, where all the tidings of the earth meet. The second book treats of the
journey in middle air, as the first treats of the starting-
point on earth, and the third treats of the destination.
What is lacking, however, is unity of mood and a strong
sense of direction throughout all three books.

The third book shows Fame granting worldly renown
to various groups of people and withholding it from
others quite without regard to their deserts. The poet
himself is asked if he is seeking fame. He replies

> 'Nay, for sothe, frend,' quod y;
> 'I cam noght hyder, graunt mercy[1]',
> For no such cause, by my hed!
> Sufficeth me, as I were ded,
> That no wight have my name in honde.
> I wot myself best how y stonde;
> For what I drye,[2] or what I thynke,
> I wil myselven al hyt drynke,
> Certeyn, for the more part,
> As fer forth as I kan myn art.

H.F. 1873–82

One can hardly doubt that this modest, sober inde-
pendence does indeed represent Chaucer's own attitude.
But what *is* he doing, someone asks him? 'That will I tell
thee', he says. It is to learn some new tidings, *he does not
know what*, either of love or similar glad things. His
unnamed questioner replies with another question—
'What are the tidings that you have thus brought here,
which you have heard? But no matter, I see what you
desire to hear.' This is the sort of mysterious inconse-
quentiality which makes the poem so exasperating, and
suggests either 'private jokes in panelled rooms', or that

---

[1] many thanks.   [2] endure.

Chaucer never really worked out what he wanted to say. However, he is taken to the House of Twigs which is the House of Fame in its other sense of Rumour, where he is to see such strange sights and hear such new things as will console him for the distress he has endured so cheerfully, having been so empty of all bliss since Fortune destroyed his heart's rest. It is the Eagle who tells him all this, thus harking back to the earlier passage where the poet was told of Jupiter's pity. His sadness may be due to the frustration of his poetry caused by the pressure of business which ties him to his office accounts all day when he would prefer to be reading. At least, strange sights and 'tidings', whether these be 'news' or 'stories', would seem to be a rather more satisfactory reward for one who was denied freedom and learning, than for one who was unlucky in love. The poet goes about inquiring eagerly for certain news—which he hints is now known pretty widely (another puzzle)—when there is suddenly a rush to one corner of the hall. A man of great authority steps forth . . . and the poem breaks off. What message the man of authority could have delivered has never been generally agreed. It seems quite possible that it also eluded Chaucer. The poem must have been very near its end; it has suddenly risen to a climax, demanding a really striking announcement, yet there seems really nothing that could have been satisfactory, for the poem is a poor prelude to any item of news in the Court. Several times when Chaucer composed a poem for which no source or analogue has been found, he failed to finish it. Like Shakespeare he seems to have found it hard to invent a plot—unlike Shakespeare, he sometimes rashly ventured to embark without this necessary chart.

It seems likely that Chaucer's purposes were confused. He started out to write a love-vision. But the real driving

force of his writing at this time was a sense of dissatisfaction which he sought to dispel. He was seeking some
new thing, some new information. An easy, conventional
melancholy was often the basis of the court-poems he
knew, and of some of the short conventional love-poems
he wrote. But in *The House of Fame* Chaucer wears his rue
with a difference. If his dissatisfaction is connected with
love how different it is from the complaints of an unsuccessful lover. He had expressed some discontent in one
or two other poems probably written before *The House
of Fame*, for example, the *Complaint unto Pity*, 99–104, and
A Complaint to his Lady, 43–5. Here he plainly refers to
unsuccessful love. The poems are conventional—Pity is
dead in his lady's heart, and the poet bewails his lot.
They may have been dedicated to a great lady, but at all
events they are not the kind of poem which conveys a
serious personal distress; they are rather 'periphrastic
studies in a worn-out poetical fashion'. Precisely the
same turn of thought as is found in these two poems re-
appears in the *Parliament*:

> For bothe I hadde thyng which that I nolde
> And ek I nadde that thing that I wolde.

P.F. 90–1

It may be doubted if this time he refers to his personal
misfortune in love. The idea itself comes from Boethius,
where Philosophy asks if this is not usually the situation
of a man's life; what he wishes for is the Good, however
he conceives it, and what he has is discontent? (III prose 3.)

The *Parliament* and *The House of Fame* have in common
the poet's melancholy and his spirit of inquiry. In each
the poet hopes to find out something, in the latter from
hearing tales, in the former from reading books. Each is
a love-vision, but neither seems to be a poem from a

lover to his mistress. Each is in a sense a philosophical poem. The *Parliament* has also its humour, but it is far less flippant than *The House of Fame*.

The *Parliament* begins with the poet's expression of his astonishment at the 'wonderful working' of love. He says that he himself knows not love in deed, yet often in books he reads of love's 'miracles and cruel ire'. Whatever the latent irony, if any, in this stanza, it places the poet in that position of an impartial sympathetic observer which he is so fond of in all his later poetry. He goes on to describe a book which had so fascinated him that for a whole day he read it both fast and eagerly 'a certeyn thing to lerne', though what he wished to learn he does not say. The book was Cicero's *Dream of Scipio*, commented upon by Macrobius, and its subject 'heaven and hell and earth, and the souls that dwell in them'. It tells how Scipio Africanus showed his grandson in a dream all the beauty of the heavens and the nothingness of earth:

> Than bad he hym, syn[1] erthe was so lyte,[2]
> And ful of torment and of harde grace,
> That he ne shulde hym in the world delyte.
>
> P.F. 64–6

Africanus says that in order to get to heaven, a man must know himself immortal, and work for the 'common profit'. There is no word of love, and since Chaucer has begun the poem by telling how love interests him, it is not surprising that he says he left his reading at night disappointed and unsuccessful in his search, 'filled with anxiety and busy heaviness'.

This introduction is structurally similar to that of *The Book of the Duchess* and *The House of Fame*, and as in them, it is followed by a dream. But first the poet invokes

[1] since.   [2] little.

'Cytherea'. He uses this title for Venus only three times
in all his works, and in each case appears to mean particularly the planet. (His reference here to 'north-north-
west' is an unsolved puzzle.) The planet Venus, says
Boccaccio, signifies love, friendship, affection, company,
domesticity, union between animals, the begetting of
children, the pleasures of men, as well as, if she be un-
propitious, the miseries of love. It is this planet which
is the guiding star of the poem, and there seems to be no
flippancy in the invocation.

In the dream Scipio, who gave such worthy but perhaps
unattractive advice in the book, comes to show the poet
not heaven nor hell, but a wondrous park, with a two-fold
promise on its gates; first that

> This is the wey to al good aventure,

P.F. 131

but also, just opposite,

> Th' eschewing is only the remedye.

P.F. 140

The park is most deliciously described. This section is
largely translated from Boccaccio's *Teseide*, and it is
interesting to see how Chaucer improves on his original,
making Boccaccio's abstract words flower into colourful,
lively images. It is a lovely garden refreshed by light
sweet breezes and the ravishing melodies of birds; it is
adorned with blossomy boughs, green meadows, flowers
white, blue, yellow and red—an Earthly Paradise. It
symbolizes for us the bright expectant springtime of young
life and love; clearly, also, it stands for the whole created
world, and the birds which later appear symbolize both
human society and all created beings.

After describing the temperate freshness of the whole

park, where there is no 'grievance of hot nor cold', no night nor bitter weather, and no man is old or sick, the dreamer sees Cupid with his followers, Pleasance, Aray, Lust, disfigured Craft, and so forth. Behind these is the temple of Venus, the mother of hot desire. Her temple, in contrast to the freshness outside, is filled with sighs and rich with a thousand sweet odours. Priapus, the lustful god, stands 'in sovereyn place', shameful, ludicrous, obscene,

> In swiche aray as whan the asse hym shente
> With cri by nighte, and with hys sceptre in honde.
>
> P.F. 255–6

Venus lies in a 'private corner', all but naked. She disports herself with Richesse who, according to the English *Romaunt* (5993 ff.), will have nothing to do with poor young men, who are the stable and steadfast lovers Cupid is lord of. On the walls of the temple are painted stories of those who have suffered bitterly for love. Infatuated and betrayed love, sometimes illicit, is portrayed everywhere—though rather as a misfortune than as a crime. Chaucer adds to the *Teseide's* list of lovers some of those placed by Dante in Hell in the Circle of the Lustful—Dido, Cleopatra, Helen, Achilles, Paris, Tristram. Troilus also is added to these sufferers, without a hint from Dante or Boccaccio.

The temple of Venus therefore shows love only as infatuation, lust, shame, misery, betrayal—indeed, as a justification of Scipio's condemnation of the world. Should any doubt of this exist in the mind of a modern reader, we may refer to Boccaccio's own *Chiose* or notes, issued with the *Teseide*. It does not seem likely now that Chaucer's copy of the *Teseide* contained these notes, but a later age may be grateful for the guidance they give to the general effect Boccaccio aimed at. The *Chiose* devote pages to the significance of the Cupid-and-Venus passage, attributing allegorical meaning to every detail. It may be doubted whether Chaucer would have been much interested in this excessive allegory of the New Learning, but there was no doubt about the general implications of the Temple of Venus. Boccaccio says

> Venus is two-fold; by the first can be and should be under-stood every honest and legitimate desire, such as to desire a wife in order to have children, and desires similar to this; and this Venus is not meant here. The second Venus is she through whom all lasciviousness is desired, and who is commonly called the goddess of love; and *she it is* whose temple and other qualities belonging to it are described here by the author, as appears in the text.[1]

Chaucer makes no overt comment on this ill-omened temple, but walks out to comfort himself. One imagines the pleasure of the fresh air again, after the scented warmth inside. So far he has seen little to assuage his discontent. However, he now sees

> a queene
> That, as of lyght the somer sonne shene
> Passeth the sterre, right so over mesure
> She fayrer was than any creature.
>
> P.F. 298–301

This is St. Valentine's day, when every bird must choose his mate at the council held by the great Queen, Nature. All the birds are present, so many of them that the dreamer has scarcely space to stand (one of Chaucer's realistic touches), and they are all in their proper degree, from the noble hawks to the plebeian cuckoo and goose. Nature, the 'vicar', or deputy, of almighty

[1] G. Boccaccio, *Teseide*, a cura di A. Roncaglia, Bari, 1941, pp. 417 ff.

God, commands them to begin to choose their mates, and he that is most worthy shall begin. There is only one condition—that whoever is chosen is not to be constrained against her will. Then the famous debate begins, for the three noblest birds who speak first all love the same formel eagle. They speak in the high-flown language of love—they address the beloved not as a mate, but as a 'sovereign lady'—they humble themselves to the dust before her, claiming rather her pity than her love, though they are fierce enough towards each other. They all claim the reward of the lady's love, one in particular for his truth, one for the length of time of his service, one for the intensity of his devotion. But their argument goes on for so long that the lower orders, who cannot choose before their natural lords have done so, become impatient. Eventually certain birds are chosen to give their opinion as to who should have the formel: the spokesmen are the noble falcon, the 'unnatural' cuckoo, the turtle-dove loyal in love till death, the vulgar and stupid goose. Their speeches are masterpieces of dramatic truth and variety—noble, selfish, loving, foolish, according to the speaker, and tinglingly alive. But their speeches are no help, and Nature gives it to the formel eagle to decide for herself—though Nature's advice is that she should choose the royal tercel, as the noblest. The formel, however, asks for a year's grace, and so the problem is postponed. The other birds then choose their mates, and fly happily away after singing in honour of Nature the lovely roundel:

Now welcome somer with thy sonne softe.

The poet awakes, and betakes himself to other books, always hoping that some day he will meet something by which he will 'fare the better'. He makes no other comment, and there is no certainty that he has resolved the problem which haunted him at the beginning.

We can now, however, at least see something of the terms of the problem. Just as the Temple of Venus represented lascivious love, so Nature represents legitimate love. The figure of Nature is the key to the latter part of the poem. She is God's deputy

> That hot, cold, hevy, lyght, moyst and dreye
> Hath knyt by evene noumbres of acord.
>
> P.F. 380–1

She knits together the diverse elements of the world by the bond of Love, as Boethius explains in the *Consolation*. Nature here is the expression of God's creative activity. Whatever she ordains is good. And love, pleasant love, is what she ordains when she tells the birds (representing all living beings) how,

> Ye knowe wel how, seynt Valentynes day
> *By my statut and thorgh my governaunce*
> Ye come for to cheese[1]—and fle youre wey—
> Youre makes,[2] *as I prike you with pleasaunce*
>
> P.F. 386–9

Yet Africanus (and a good many others including Boethius) had commanded medieval man

> That he ne shulde hym in the world delyte.

Here is an important contrast of authorities in the poem. Another important contrast lies within the garden of love itself, between good love and corrupted love; Nature and Venus.

The poem thus presents first the major problem of the dualism of the world, then the subsidiary comment on the two kinds of love. We see these not in terms of

[1] choose.   [2] mates.

logical conflict, but rather as masses of light and shade are balanced against each other in a picture.

The love-debate itself has its conflicts and contrasts, too, some of them set within each other, like a Chinese box puzzle. There is the social conflict—easily enough appreciated in the turbulent years before and after the Peasants' Revolt. We cannot doubt here where the poet's convictions lie, for it is Nature (i.e. by implication, God) who ordains the ranks of society. There is also, on the most obvious level, the fashionable *demande d'amour*—who should win the formel? There is yet another question, inherent in the contest between the suitors—the paradox of love itself as set forth on the gates of the park. Love causes both happiness and unhappiness. In large part, the unhappiness of love is caused by the lascivious Venus—love unrestrained by modesty. But even under Nature there is unhappiness. She is good, and gives us instincts which it is both our pleasure and our duty to satisfy. Yet even in following Nature there may be frustration and unhappiness, as there must be for the unsuccessful suitors. The irony is that this afflicts pre-eminently the noblest and worthiest. The lower orders, with their coarse lack of sensibility, their desire primarily for a mate, find no such frustration, and depart happily. Chaucer puts the problem even more plainly in another Valentine poem of the same period—that witty, though arid poem, *The Complaint of Mars.*

> To what fyn[1] made the God that sit so hye,
> Benethen him, love other companye,
> *And streyneth[2] folk to love, malgre[3] hir hed[3]?* . . .
> Hit semeth He hath to lovers enmyte,
> And lyk a fissher, as men alday may se

[1] end.   [2] constrains.   [3] in spite of their own wish.

Baiteth hys angle-hok *with som pleasaunce*,
Til many a fissh ys wod[1] til that he be
Sesed therwith; and then at erst[2] hath he
Al his desyr, and therwith all myschaunce.

218 . . . 241

What, however, is the total effect in the *Parliament*?
Chaucer, like other medieval writers of debates, deliberately leaves the problem open—he is no propagandist.
But the satirical humour of parts of the debate should
not blind us to the genuine seriousness beneath. The
strain between the two ways of life, the way of Acceptance, the way of Denial, he does not finally resolve till
the end of his life, when, old and tired, he takes the way
of Denial and condemns his non-religious writings. But
in this fruitful period of manhood, conscious of and
delighting in his powers and the richness of the world, he
very strongly leans towards the way of Acceptance.
Nature is good, and genuine love is good, since ordained
by her—that is the overwhelming impression left by the
Parliament.

Chaucer himself called the poem *The Parlement of
Fowles* and the debate has always and rightly been
thought the heart of the poem. The whole poem is
itself as it were a debate about the nature of love, though
the movement of thought is by association and contrast,
rather than by direct logic. *The Dream of Scipio* gives a
world-picture in which the world is despised—a view
of great authority in Chaucer's day. By contrast, the
park of Nature represents the world as God's own
creation, and under His law. Within the park the
pictorial or dramatic descriptions of Venus and the
noble and common birds all show contrasting aspects of
or attitudes to love. It is typical of Chaucer's method of

[1] mad.   [2] first.

writing poetry that he presents these contrasts in the form of descriptions with a high degree of surface decoration, and that he leaves an appreciation of them and of the underlying principle of connexion to the reader's wit and imagination. He creates a set of 'states of feeling' which interact and come to fruition in the reader's own mind. He does not argue a case—it is no lecture on love's philosophy. Even the birds' arguments are more dramatic than logical; they are contrasts in attitudes. Although the ostensible subject of debate is who should marry the formel, the real subject of what the common birds say is the nature and value of love. And the delightful comedy of their argument only enhances the genuine seriousness of the fundamental issues. *The Parliament* is beyond question the richest and most remarkable poem of its length in the English language.[1]

---

[1] See further *The Parlement of Foulys*, ed. D. S. Brewer, 2nd impression, 1961 (in Nelson's Medieval and Renaissance Library).

Chapter Seven

THE ROMANCES

IT seems likely that Chaucer's next poem was the *Palamon and Arcite*, later used for the *Knight's Tale*. In some respects it is less ambitious than *The House of Fame* and the *Parliament*, in that Chaucer has taken a particular story rather than a general theme. From now on, indeed, Chaucer tells stories, and philosophical themes arise only incidentally. He has found his true manner at last. The rather curious constructions of the *Parliament* and *The House of Fame* are no more repeated. His stories, however, do not lose in richness what they gain in simplicity. The precepts of the rhetoricians had amply instructed him in the art of loading every rift with ore. Description and comment arise in connection with the fates and characters of particular men and women, and the philosophical implications are more easily manageable when so introduced.

However, in the *Knight's Tale*, as it may still be called by a convenient anachronism, there are still a few elements not entirely dissolved into the narrative stream, notably the descriptions of the Temples of Venus, Mars and Diana. Hence, perhaps, a few inconsistencies.[1] It is

---

[1] The long descriptions of the temples, with their mythological and astrological significances, impede the narrative, and are perhaps liable to bore the reader anxious to get on with the story. Chaucer was elsewhere also willing to sacrifice the flow of narrative in order to bring out certain themes in the story. Examples are Troilus's long soliloquy on predestination (*Troilus*, IV, 946 ff.), and the discourse on *gentilesse* in *The Wife of Bath's Tale* (*Canterbury Tales*, III (D), 1109 ff.); and there are several others. Probably Chaucer was also tempted by his pleasure in the subjects for their own sakes.

also still a poem about love rather than lovers, and the characters are not much individualised. The poem dwells on one subject, the love of the two young men for Emily, and only what relates strictly to this is told. The romance selects one or two of the more gorgeous of the various strands of life, and weaves a simpler pattern than we find in our everyday existence. There is both advantage and loss in this. We lose the sense of immediacy. We gain in pure beauty. Because there are few of those half-tones and neutral colours which make up so much of ordinary life, the contrasts are more striking. Everything is heightened, all elements are purer, better or worse than in life. Joy is unalloyed, sorrow unalleviated. Everything is simpler and more intense, and because of this we see more deeply into the nature of love—or of a certain kind of love—than we should have done had we not seen it in isolation.

The *Knight's Tale* has some close resemblances to the *Parliament*. The Temple of Venus appears : there are two rival suitors, of almost identical merit, for the hand of a maiden, who though she would prefer virginity is quite resigned to marry the suitor fate will prefer. Both suitors reverence their lady, and their love is honourable ; its aim is marriage. The same poem of Boccaccio's, the *Teseide*, which provided material for the *Parliament*, is the basis of the *Knight's Tale*. The later poem represents a further stage in the adaptation of Italian material.

The *Teseide* is the first of the modern epics—that form which bedevilled the European literary mind from the fifteenth to the eighteenth centuries, and which hampered even Milton's genius. The recipe for it was, Copy the *Aeneid*. The *Teseide* suffers from its servility. It is a slender story padded out to epic length. Chaucer, untouched by the arrogance of the New Learning, saw better than Boccaccio what the material was worth, borrowed much description and the central plot, and turned the whole thing back into Romance. At the same time he learnt from his Italian reading the merits of construction and a certain broadness of scope in narration. He 'padded' his story, just as Boccaccio did, but the 'padding'—the comment and description—is less extensive, and is relevant to the themes innate in the story. Chaucer cut out almost the whole account of Theseus's wars, and concentrated on the story of the friendship of Palamon and Arcite, who became prisoners of Theseus for life. He tells how their love for Emily destroys their friendship; how they regained their freedom and served long and faithfully for love; he describes their battle for Emily and the great tournament; and finally Arcite's death and Palamon's eventual marriage to Emily.

The glory of the *Knight's Tale* lies in the splendour and vividness of description—of Emily the bright, of May morning, of the tournament—and in the nobility of sentiment. Chaucer hardly descends from the rather rarefied atmosphere to suggest the daily intercourse of common life, yet the varied events are related with a wealth of accurate and realistic detail, from the dimensions of the lists and behaviour of the crowd, to the diagnosis of Arcite's injuries. As generalized as the characters are, they too have their appropriate qualities. Arcite is more ruthless, more arrogant than his rival. It is he who arraigns the gods when he suffers the pangs of love. Palamon, who saw Emily first, is more humble, more reverent. There is also humour—most noticeably in Theseus's speech when he finds the two lovers fighting for a lady who is entirely ignorant of the existence of both. Anyone who thinks from this (or from the goose's arguments in the *Parliament*) that Chaucer really thought love foolish, has not begun to understand him. But Chaucer would have been foolish himself had he not seen that love, looked at from outside—in the dullness of age, or in clownish ignorance—often seems absurd, like other fine feelings. By admitting such criticism into his poems he so to speak, neutralizes it, deals with it on his own ground, and at the same time widens the scope of his own work. There are also such slight touches of flippancy, as his comment on the destination of souls; or his remark about Emily, that

> wommen as to speken in comune
> Thei folwen alle the favour of Fortune,
>
> I (A), 2681-2

which are characteristic, and which jar unpleasantly.

The great theme is Love, and a *demande d'amour* arises here as in the *Parliament*. However, in this case the problem is solved by Death, which thus appears for the second time in Chaucer's verse. Both Love and Death are the subjects of high poetry.

Love is ruled by Destiny:

> For certeinly, oure appetites heer
> Be it of werre, of pees, or hate, or love,
> Al is this reuled by the sighte above.
>
> I (A), 1670-2

In this poem Chaucer does not touch the profounder depths implied by this belief. He is more concerned to show the nobleness of love,

> That is to seyn, trouthe, honour, and knyghthede
> Wysdom, humblesse, estaat, and heigh kynrede,
> Fredom,[1] and al that longeth to that art.
>
> I (A), 2789-91

[1] generosity.

Since he is consciously writing an historical romance, about pagans, he represents them worshipping pagan divinities—whose supposed powers, as he well knew, were really those of the planets bearing indeed names of gods, but actually channels of the true God's divine purpose. Thus he describes Palamon as praying

> Unto the blisful Citherea benigne
> I mene Venus, honurable and digne,

I (A), 2215

although her temple is that described in the *Teseide*, of the lascivious Venus, of which Chaucer condenses the description, and leaves out most of its wantonness.[1]

From the contemplation of the 'fair chain of Love' Theseus, in the great speech on the death of Arcite, passes to the inevitable transitoriness of all things; the First Mover he says, having established the chain of love to bind all things together, has also set a limited duration to all things; all things must pass away.

> What maketh this but Juppiter, the kyng,
> The which is prince and cause of alle thyng,
> Convertynge al unto his propre welle[2]
> From which it is dirryved,[3] sooth to telle?
> And heer-agayns no creature on lyve,
> Of no degree, availleth for to stryve.
>   Thanne is it wysdom, as it thynketh me,
> To maken vertu of necessitee . . .
> *Why grucchen[4] heere his cosyn and his wyf*
> *Of his welfare, that loved hem so weel?*
> Kan he hem thank? Nay, God woot, never a deel,

[1] All three deities display their powers mainly through the disasters they cause. This is perhaps to be related to the notable pessimism of the later Middle Ages throughout Europe. Huizinga points out that by this time the saints who were once regarded as the protectors against disaster were now often regarded, by an easy transition of thought, as having the disasters within their power, to be released or not, accordingly as they were propitiated.

[2] will.   [3] derived.   [4] begrudge.

That both his soule *and eek hemself offende,*
And yet they mowe[1] hir lustes[2] nat amende.
    What may I conclude of this longe serye,[3]
But after wo I rede[4] us to be merye,
And thanken Juppiter of al his grace?
And er that we departen from this place
I rede[4] that we make of sorwes two
O[5] parfit joye, lastynge everemo.

I (A), 3035 . . . 72

Death, says Theseus, is natural and must be accepted:
it is a return to the fountain-head of all good, and no dead
man will thank us for mourning for something which is
really his welfare. There can be no final tragedy for any
good man. Let us resign ourselves to the will of God,
subject ourselves without repining to the necessary conditions and ups-and-downs of existence, making the best of
misery, and thanking God for his great mercies. Thus
here, as in the *Parliament*, and (in my opinion) as is implied by the end of the *Troilus*, Chaucer values the world
in itself, but 'despises' it from the point of view of
Heaven. It is a 'foul prison' (*Knight's Tale*, 3061), a
'wretched world' (*Troilus*, V. 1817), looked at from
Heaven; but it is 'ruled by the sight above', and it is
our duty cheerfully to make the best of it.

On reading this speech, and others of its kind elsewhere in Chaucer's verse, we may well say with Milton

> How charming is divine philosophy,
> Not harsh and crabbed, as dull fools suppose.

The speech is not merely the versification of somewhat
trite philosophy. It has the authentic poetic blend of
thought and feeling in musical verse. The exalted conception of life rouses that unique sense of philosophical

---

[1] may.   [2] desires.   [3] series.   [4] advise.   [5] one.

and aesthetic satisfaction which is the product of true metaphysical poetry. Compassion and understanding unite to beget delight. Its position in the story augments the power of the speech, and our interest in what Theseus says is strengthened by our interest in the fates of Palamon and Arcite.

This serene acceptance crowns the nobility of the *Knight's Tale*. It seems to be Chaucer's own reply to the problem of evil, even if it can hardly be called a solution. Here is the spiritual basis of Chaucer's poetry, of his pathos and of his comedy, too.

The most profound and moving treatment of love, however, is in the *Troilus*, which is the peak of the achievements of these years. The poem is a tragedy, which according to Chaucer's gloss in the *Consolation* 'is to seyn a dite of prosperite for a tyme, that endith in wrecchidnesse'—worldly wretchedness, that is to say, for it will be well to bear in mind Theseus's (and Chaucer's) view that there can be no *final* tragedy for a good man, since he goes to Heaven.

The poem is divided into five books, each book prefaced by an invocation. Chaucer uses these invocations (usually based on hints from Boccaccio and Dante) with magnificent effect to set the atmosphere of each book. Nothing shows better Chaucer's command of the 'high style' where he feels it justified, than the beauty and power of these beginnings. Obviously he had considered the form of his poem, according to the best precepts of the rhetoricians; the very process is described in a passage actually translated from Geoffroi de Vinsauf (the rhetorician he knew best):

> For everi wight that hath an hous to founde
> Ne renneth, naught the werk for to bygynne

With rakel[1] hond, but he wol bide a stounde,[2]
And sende his hertes line out fro withinne
Alderfirst his purpos for to wynne.

I. 1065–9

Medieval rhetoric has been unnecessarily despised. Its
principles were good, although they were sometimes, as
it seems to us, absurdly elaborated. Chaucer's remould-
ing of the story of Troilus to suit his own purposes was
entirely in accordance with rhetorical teaching. Further
evidence of Chaucer's anxious care over the *Troilus* is the
fact that he revised it at least twice, probably in 1384–5.
With each revision he deepened the philosophical tone
and implications of the poem, making such additions as
Troilus's long soliloquy in the temple about predestination and free will (IV. 946 ff.). The revisions are not
mere after-thoughts, touchings-up—they are all intended
to draw out the significance of the events related. The
additions do not add to the colour or detail of the
setting, or extend the portrayal of character.

The seriousness with which Chaucer treated his poem
is probably due to the fact that he regarded it as history.
Medieval poets did not consider poetry to be something
set apart, and historians sometimes wrote in verse. The
immediate source of the *Troilus* is the *Filostrato*, another
poem by Boccaccio (whom Chaucer calls Lollius for no
known reason). Boccaccio invented the actual plot
which Chaucer took over, but found his raw material in
the Tróy-books of earlier writers, Benoît de Sainte-
Maure, Guido delle Colonne, and Joseph of Exeter.
Chaucer too consulted these older writers, and also references to Troy in such authors as Ovid and Statius. Whenever he diverges from Boccaccio in a matter of *fact* it is
usually because he is following a more ancient authority.

[1] rash.   [2] while.

Because the *Troilus* is historical, like the *Knight's Tale*, Chaucer makes an attempt to recapture something of the flavour of antiquity. He makes this clear at the beginning of Book II when he says that in the course of a thousand years words and customs change greatly,

> Ek in som lond were al the game shent
> If that they ferde in love *as men don here*,
> *As thus, in opyn doyng*, or in chere,
> In visityng, in forme, or seyde hir sawes.
> Forthi men seyn, ecch contree hath his lawes.
>
> II. 38–42

The secrecy of the love-affair, the manner of its conduct, are not to be thought of as representing the customs of fourteenth-century England. The plot is set in a far country, many years ago, in pagan times.

Nevertheless, it was impossible for the fourteenth century to imagine a time or a society greatly different from its own. The historical imagination was not fully developed till the nineteenth century. So Chaucer's picture of Troy is really a picture of medieval London with its city walls, tight-packed houses and many gardens, and also with its fear of the enemy without, its alarms, its chains across the streets. One of the most remarkable qualities of the poem is the sense of city-life, of many people moving about, of the real world. There is the feeling of daily life which Chaucer excluded from the *Knight's Tale*. We see Criseyde being read to in her parlour. We walk with her and her maidens out of the house into her orderly, well-kept garden where the walks are all railed,

> And shadewed wel with blosmy bowes grene,
> And benched newe, and sonded alle the weyes.
>
> II. 821–2

The story is held in the network of social relationships.
It is at a supper-party of nobles that Criseyde is first
brought to meet Troilus. It is an afternoon visit from
ladies, friends of Criseyde's, which brings out most
acutely her agony at the coming separation, the irony of
her position, her pathetic isolation. Their congratulations,
their chattering, drive her to tears of distraction, while

> thilke[1] fooles sittynge hire aboute
> Wenden[2] that she wepte and siked[3] sore
> Bycause that she sholde out of that route[4]
> Departe, and never pleye with hem more.
>
> IV. 715–18

Nor does Chaucer neglect the romantic beauty of night
in the medieval city; as Criseyde meditates on the tidings
of love:

> A nyghtyngale, upon a cedir grene,
> Under the chambre wal ther as she ley
> Ful loude song ayein the moone shene,
> Peraunter,[5] in his briddes wise, a lay
> Of love, that made hire herte fressh and gay.
> That herkned she so longe in good entente,
> Till at the laste the dede[6] slep hire hente.[7]
>
> II. 918–24

Or again, after the first bitter night of Troilus's endur-
ance of Criseyde's absence:

> On hevene yet the sterres weren seene,
> Although ful pale ywoxen[8] was the moone;
> And whiten gan the orisonte[9] shene
> Al estward, as it wont is for to doone;
> And Phebus with his rosy carte soone
> Gan[10] after that to dresse hym up to fare,
> When Troilus hath sent after Pandare.
>
> V. 274–80

| [1] those. | [2] thought. | [3] sighed. | [4] company. | [5] perhaps. |
| [6] dead. | [7] carried off. | [8] become. | [9] horizon. | [10] began. |

The somewhat austere beauty of this description is so precise that we almost feel the cool dawn wind on our faces. The use of the mythological Phoebus for the sun, after the bare accuracy of the earlier lines, brings colour and light, brightens the stanza, just as the red flush of dawn brightens the pallor of the night sky. We are conscious of the continuing revolution of night and day about the earth, its-beauty and at the same time its calm usualness. Yet for all its freshness and immediacy, the stanza draws heavily on the *Teseide*, and is not without reminiscences of Boethius and Statius.

All this, however, is no more than the setting: the central characters and their story are what engage mind and heart. The characters are almost entirely Chaucer's own creation; he took no more than hints from Boccaccio. Pandarus is the most original. Probably, as Mr. Coghill suggests, the change from Pandaro the colourless go-between of the *Filostrato* to this older courtier and man of the world, with his 'impishness and deep, almost sensual affection for his Prince', arose from Chaucer's different conception of the story. As has been said, medieval poets respected what they regarded as the facts or plot of a story; they felt themselves entirely free to give their own interpretation of them.[1] The *Filostrato* is a story of straightforward sexual passion. The *Troilus* is a story about truth and untruth in love, with wide implications. The nobility of Chaucer's main characters includes an almost excessively refined modesty. Boccaccio's Troilo, well experienced in love-affairs, could do his own wooing for himself. Chaucer's Troilus needs

[1] This important distinction between plot or 'matter', and presentation or interpretation in medieval literary theory is made clear in Professor E. Vinaver's most valuable introduction to *The Works of Sir Thomas Malory*, 1947. Professor J. W. H. Atkins, *English Literary Criticism; Medieval*, 1943, makes the same point.

someone to do his wooing for him. Pandarus is the
man. The wooing once accomplished, his activity in the
plot is finished. He becomes little more than the confi-
dant and foil to Troilus, setting off Troilus's nobility and
lack of worldly wisdom. The character of Pandarus
therefore needed to be that of an ingenious, sympathetic
and authoritative person, who should also be a companion
to Troilus. Chaucer therefore makes him uncle to
Criseyde (not cousin, as Troilo is) and a courtier in the
royal household attached by the strongest ties of loyalty
and comradeship to his young prince. There were inconsistencies inherent in such a conception. We feel Pandarus to be a good deal older than Troilus and yet he is
the closest of comrades to this very young man; Chaucer
carefully omits to tell us anything of his age.[1] But never
did a character become more instantly alive than does
Pandarus. It is by his conversation that he at once finds
a place in our hearts and memories. Chaucer's power of
dramatic characterization is here shown to the full.
Pandarus reveals his subtlety and devotion with his very
first words, when he hears Troilus bewailing his misery
and immediately pours sarcasm upon his head.

> Thise wordes seyde he for the nones alle,
> That with swich thing he myght hym angry maken,
> And with an angre[2] don[3] his wo to falle.[4]
>
> I. 561–3

When Troilus tells him of his despairing love for Cris-

[1] Most of our older writers took their story first, constructing their characters in accordance with the demands of their interpretation of the plot,
rather than allowing the story to arise out of their conception of a character,
as is the general custom of more modern novelists. When the story comes
first it occasionally forces inconsistencies upon the character, as sometimes
happens in Shakespeare—e.g. between the character and his actions, as with
Bassanio, and, perhaps, Othello; or in a character himself at different stages
of the action, as with Hamlet. But the main thing is that the character should
have power to convince us while he is before our eyes, in the limited context
of the immediate scene.   [2] fit of anger.   [3] cause.   [4] cease.

eyde, Pandarus 'well nigh melts' for woe and pity—
and is immediately ready with busy stratagems, exhorta-
tions to bear up, disquisitions on the nature of love, and
all the worldly wisdom of a multitude of proverbs. He
understands the nature of men and women—the way he
later leads on Criseyde's curiosity is a delight to see—he
knows all the usages of love and how to conduct a love-
affair. His friendship for Troilus, his guardianship of
Criseyde are brimming with emotion—a characteristically fourteenth-century blend of sensibility and senti-
mentality, with the tears always near the surface. There
is no one better than he at the management of any kind of
affairs—except, apparently, his own. He is like the man
who always wins when he gambles with other people's
money, and always loses with his own. Perhaps the final
masterliness of Chaucer's conception of Pandarus lies in
this, and in the wry humour with which Pandarus regards
his own lack of success in love. His humour is a little
different from the gaiety, never obtrusive, which is the
mark of his social ease and good breeding, and different
from his occasional facetiousness which reminds us of an
old-fashioned uncle's jokes at a wedding or christening.
Pandarus's humour corresponds with Chaucer's own
occasional (and sometimes unfortunate) flippancy. It
turns his own unsuccess into a family joke. It would, if it
could, do the same for Troilus's loss of Criseyde. There
is a vein of harsh cynicism in it, a deep-rooted scepticism,
to be seen in particular in Book V, where he becomes a
foil to Troilus's noble constancy; thus while Troilus is
still deceiving himself with hope,

> Pandare answerde, 'It may be, wel ynough,'
> And held with hym of al that evere he seyde.
> But in his herte he thoughte, and softe lough[1]

[1] laughed.

And to hymself ful sobreliche he seyde,
'From haselwode, there joly Robyn pleyde,
Shal come al that that thow abidest heere.
Ye, fare wel al the snow of ferne[1] yere!'

V. 1170–6

He is quite right, of course, Criseyde will never come
back. Pandarus sees clearly enough 'this world's transmutations'. What he does not see is the permanence
which underlies them. In a word, he lacks any religious
sense. This is quite untrue of Chaucer, and for this
reason it is impossible to agree with some critics who
suggest that Pandarus is largely an unconscious self-
portrait of Chaucer himself, whatever superficial simi-
larities he and Chaucer may be thought to share.

Pandarus and Criseyde share at least this family like-
ness: they are both entirely moulded by the society
which surrounds them and by the events which affect
them. Since Criseyde is gone, Pandarus easily adjusts
himself to the new situation. Troilus not merely cannot,
he will not. His devotion has a religious and transcendental fervour (indeed, there are elements in it which only a
Kierkegaard or a Kafka could have brought out). Criseyde, tender and timid, takes her colour from her situation. She is a widow, a proud young beauty, who, when
the poem begins, is fully content with her state. Pandarus declares Troilus's love, and keeps his image before
her mind. She falls in love, but does nothing of herself.
Once her fears have been reasoned away, she lets herself
be urged gently towards the consummation of her love
with no more than token resistance. When she and
Troilus have become lovers she is again content with her
new situation until forced away, 'with wommen few,
among the Grekes strong'. There the 'sudden Diomede'

[1] last.

speedily assuages her grief. She entertains his proposals
for reasons similar to those which had first favoured
Troilus before she loved him, for there is a vein of cool
calculation in Criseyde. She reflects upon Diomede's
power and importance, 'the peril of the town' to which
she has rashly promised to return, and her own need for
protection. She vows a similar vow of faithfulness:

> To Diomede algate I wol be trewe.
>
> V. 1071

With a noble lover she remained noble. With Diomede
she can descend to the shameful deceit of her letters to
Troilus; letters which give false reasons for her delay in
returning to him, and which even reproach him for his
impatience.

Yet what a charming heroine she is. Her warm and
tender femininity, her sweet playfulness, her youthful and
ingenuous timidity, contrast effectively and convincingly
with her dignity as a great lady, when for example, we
first see her in the temple, her golden-haired beauty set
off by her black widow's dress. She stands modestly
and unaccompanied, but her bearing alone reveals her
'honour, estate, and womanly noblesse', and she in-
spires a proper respect,

> for she let falle
> Hire look a lite aside in swich manere,
> Ascaunces, 'What! may I nat stonden here?'
>
> I. 290–2

Chaucer loves her, and tells the story of her final desertion
with obvious pain and reluctance:

> Ne me[1] ne list[1] this sely[2] womman chyde
> Forther than the storye wol devyse.
> Hire name, allas! is punysshed so wide,

[1] It does not please me.   [2] wretched.

That for hire gilt it oughte ynough suffise.
And if I myghte excuse hire any wise,
For she so sory was for hire untrouthe,
Iwis,[1] I wolde excuse hire yet for routhe.[2]

V. 1093–9

His pity softens the hard outlines of her treachery.
Chaucer does not, of course, analyse character, he presents it dramatically; and none of his portraits is more
subtle and alive than Criseyde's. We seem to see into her
very heart. The movements of mind that carry her to
the supreme happiness of her love for Troilus, and to her
degrading acceptance of Diomede are entirely convincing.
Only thus, we feel, could such events have occurred.
Boccaccio, it seems, must have been wrong about her.
Chaucer sums up her character, along with those of
Troilus and Diomede, just before the betrayal. It is here
he calls her 'tendre-herted, slydynge of corage'—a detail
suggested not by Boccaccio but by Benoît and Guido
(whom, being more ancient, Chaucer would have regarded as more authoritative), and from which springs
the whole difference between Chaucer's and Boccaccio's
conception of her character.

It has been suggested that had Criseyde not been forced
to face so harsh a test she would have lived to enjoy all
that 'which should accompany old age, As honour, love,
obedience, troops of friends'. All she needed was protection, to stay behind some walls—of Troy, or, as it
might be, of the Garden of the Rose. There she is completely in her element. She can play with the Lady Glad-
ness and the Lord Mirth; Youth, Wealth, and Beauty are
her everyday companions, with whom she may wander
and listen to romances and love-songs. But it is of the
nature of the world's transmutations that no one can stay

H   [1] certainly.   [2] pity.

in the Garden. Even if Covetousness and Poverty are excluded, Old Age will drag one out to execution, or Anger break in, as the Greeks broke into Troy. Sooner or later Criseyde would have been found out.

If Criseyde's character is the most fascinating of the three main personages, that of Troilus is the most important. The story is written, so to speak, from his point of view. As the burden of the action is carried by the heroine, so the burden of the interpretation, the philosophical implications of the story, are carried by the hero. Perhaps it is because of this that Troilus, as Mr. C. S. Lewis has said, shares something of the anonymity of the 'I', the Dreamer, of the *Roman de la Rose*. He is not a stick, but he is a character of a noble simplicity, neither complex nor ambiguous. Once in love he is the perfect lover—to borrow the praise of Sir Launcelot, the truest lover among sinful men that ever loved woman, the sternest knight to his mortal foe. Chaucer as usual gives us the fullness of concrete description of Troilus's happy activity, the honour he receives, his devotion, his gratitude, his virtue and humility, in a splendid passage of praise at the end of Book III.

Troilus reaches this superlative excellence through Love. His manliness is perhaps worth emphasizing because of the, to us, alien extravagance of his sorrows—his readiness to weep and pine. Fundamentally, this is part of Chaucer's conception of the tenderness and refinement of his nature, for in these qualities he far surpasses Pandarus. Pandarus has continually to exhort him to bear up. Troilus is no experienced man of the world. Love is not for him simply one of the many occupations of a knight. It becomes the main-spring of his existence. Like Sir Launcelot he is one of nature's aristocrats, as well as one of society's; his feelings are finer-wrought than those of his peers. We must also make other allowances. Middle-aged critics are liable to forget the tremblings of youthful love; and Englishmen were less inhibited in the fourteenth century than they are reputed to be at a later date. The English were very easily moved to tears, if we are to believe the contemporary French chronicler, Creton. And love traditionally produced violent effects. Both Sir Launcelot and Sir Tristram ran mad into the woods. In one of Chrétien's romances, a knight falls in love with one of the Queen's ladies while they are on a sea-voyage. This is not realized by the Queen, for she imputes the symptoms to sea-sickness.

Troilus expresses the usual sentiments of the lover. He is humble as well as devoted, and grants his lady full sovereignty. When he falls in love, he is bewildered by the pain.

> If love be good, from whennes cometh my woo?
>
> I. 402

When Troilus finally loses Criseyde he inveighs bitterly against Jove and Fortune. But in particular his suffering forces him to consider the nature of love, and the nature of the world which can contain such suffering. From the very start he realizes that he must love because of Destiny. In one of the revisions Chaucer gave a long and elaborate soliloquy to Troilus, when first bereft of Criseyde, where, praying in the temple, he meditates bitterly on whether we have free choice. Here Chaucer shows his supreme dramatic sense, for he does not turn Troilus into a philosopher. The philosophic argument, literally unrealistic as it may be, has poetic truth, for Troilus's musings are the fruit of his pain, and he comes to no clear conclusion about God's Providence. He achingly turns over the thoughts of the wise (Boethius is Chaucer's source) and is forced back to his original feeling that all events, including his love, are controlled by destiny. But he arrives at no philosophical acceptance of God's will. He breaks off in his grief simply to cry out in the fullness of misery

> 'Almyghty Jove in trone[1]
> That woost[2] of al this thyng the sothfastnesse,
> Rewe[3] on my sorwe, and do me deyen[4] sone,
> Or bryng Criseyde and me fro this destresse.'
>
> IV. 1079–82

He is too young and too ardent, too simple and true, to reason himself out of sorrow. Chaucer does not blink the fact of his suffering. He eases us by no exaltation of emotion in a swift death; we have to face the remorselessness of continuing life:

> Gret was the sorwe and pleynte[5] of Troilus;
> But forth hire cours Fortune ay gan to holde.
> Criseyde loveth the sone of Tideus,
> And Troilus moot[6] wepe in cares colde.
> Swich[7] is this world, whoso it kan byholde:
> In ech estat is litel hertes reste.
> God leve[8] us for to take it for the beste.
>
> V. 1744–50

But the story is greater than the characters. It is a poem about Love, as well as about lovers. The note of Destiny is continually sounded—not only by Troilus, but by Chaucer himself, whose comments extend those of Troilus. It is as if Troilus can see so far, but the author, from his superior standpoint, sees farther, though he looks in the same direction. Destiny is the same as Fortune,

[1] throne. [2] know. [3] have pity. [4] die.
[5] complaint. [6] must. [7] such. [8] grant.

as may be seen by comparing with the *Knight's Tale*
(A.1663 ff.) this from the *Troilus*:

> But O Fortune, executrice of wyrdes,[1]
> O influences of thise hevenes hye!
> Soth is, that under God ye ben our hierdes.[2]
>
> III. 617–19

This comes from the passage which tells how, whatever
her will, Criseyde inevitably goes to what is to be,
unknown to her, an assignation with Troilus. The same
Fortune governs all the world, and it is she who causes
the fall of Troy. The story of Troy, however, is here outside Chaucer's main interest, which is the inevitability of
love;

> For evere it was, and evere it shal bifalle
> That love is he that alle thing may bynde;
> *For may no man fordon[3] the lawe of kynde.*[4]
>
> I. 236–8

(Nature, in the *Parliament*, is the 'noble goddess of Kind'.
She, i.e. in theological terms, God, has ordained love.)
Pandarus also refers to the inevitability of love as a
commonplace:

> For this have I herd seyd of wyse lered,
> 'Was never man or womman yet bigete
> That was unapt to suffren loves hete
> *Celestial, or elles love of kinde'.*
>
> I. 976–9

The remark in the *Filostrato* which is the basis of this is a
merely casual cynicism of Pandaro's. There is no cynicism as it is given here, with the weight of ancient
authority, though Pandarus immediately develops it
rather casuistically.

The supreme poetic expression of Love's power is the

---

[1] fates.   [2] guardians.   [3] destroy.   [4] nature.

invocation to love at the beginning of Book III. Here
'Venus' signifies the pagan goddess (because it is a poem
about pagan times); the planet, with its influences; the
love which binds the world; and perhaps even the Holy
Spirit; though of course each plane of meaning is not
equally present in every line. Such is Chaucer's richness,
even in the naturally diffuse medium of narrative poetry.
Nor is he frigidly intellectual; the great conception
brings a grateful feeling of illumination, understanding,
and above all, delight.

It need hardly be reiterated that the poem is not a
philosophical treatise. All that is said of Love arises out
of the contemplation of the story of one man, Troilus;
what is said about Love applies to Criseyde only in so far
as she is implicated in Troilus's life. When the philosophical implications are laid bare we are inclined to ask
questions. How does the Destiny of Love affect, for
example, the relation between Criseyde and Diomede?
Chaucer does not tell us—Destiny is conspicuous by its
absence. We never feel that it was impossible for Criseyde
to return to Troy. We only see Troilus's inevitable loss.
Nor does this philosophical inconsistency or omission
matter in the least, for the situation is poetically true.
Troilus *inevitably* must lose Criseyde—for must she not
die some time? All events of the story are seen solely
from the point of view of Troilus.

It is important to emphasize the God-ordained nature
of Love as Chaucer sees it. In the fine stanzas at the
beginning of Book III he says

> God loveth, and to love wol nought werne;[1]
> And in this world no lyves creature,
> Withouten love, is worth,[2] or may endure.
>
>   III. 12–14

[1] refuse.   [2] worthy.

When Troilus and Criseyde have consummated their love, Troilus sings a song of triumphant bliss and gratitude, which celebrates human love as the highest earthly joy, ordained by God, part of the great chain which controls the whole universe. This song does not merely give Troilus's own point of view. Chaucer himself immediately goes on to praise Troilus's behaviour as inspired by Love, and to say

> For soth to seyne, he lost held every wyght
> But if he were in loves heigh servise,
> *I mene folk that oughte it ben of right.*

III. 1793–5

The only possible assumption is that Troilus 'ought it been of right' as well. But of course, according to the story, Troilus and Criseyde were *not* married. Does Chaucer here approve illicit love? Most critics have thought so. There are two arguments against this. First, the whole trend of Chaucer's thought about Love which culminates in passages already quoted from the *Troilus* itself, shows that he considered it divinely ordained. Secondly, Chaucer nowhere else celebrates illicit love. In the *Canterbury Tales* it is sometimes material for a joke; but in his serious love-poems love is always concerned with marriage. For example, in the *Legend of Good Women* every deserted lover without exception is either a wife, or has been betrayed by the promise of marriage. The love ethic of the *Knight's Tale* is another obvious example.

How then can we explain the situation in the *Troilus*? The answer is to be found in the distinction already referred to which medieval poets made between plot and interpretation. Chaucer interprets the plot *as if* Troilus and Criseyde were married. Troilus gives thanks to

Venus, 'the wel-willy planete', and to 'Imeneus'—
Hymen, the 'god of wedding'. But in the song he
obviously cannot mention 'the holy bond of matrimony'
outright. The fact is that Chaucer, throughout the poem,
obscures the illicit nature of their love. He avoids all
mention of marriage because marriage would have
ruined his plot, and because there was no warrant for
marriage in his plot as he received it. As has been said,
the story of Troilus was a matter of history to him.
He would not have felt himself free to alter the plot. He
does his best to cover up this inconsistency between plot
and interpretation by reference to ancient times and
different customs at the beginning of Book II, and by
avoiding mention of what would have emphasized it—
marriage. He did not want his readers or audience to
think about marriage. And of course he was helped here
by a tradition which did not, to say the least, closely
associate love and marriage. Such a breach between plot
and interpretation is of course an artistic blemish, but
it is not uncommon in medieval literature. If we accept
this fundamental inconsistency much that has been hitherto puzzling becomes clear. It explains why a furtive and
secret love-affair is celebrated in such uncompromising
terms of God's Providence. And it is the *interpretation*
which is important, which is Chaucer's—the story is
someone else's. Chaucer celebrates love in its fullest
glory of flesh as well as spirit, yet out of this springs
quite naturally Troilus's song of joy and gratitude to
'benign Love, thou holy bond of things', to Venus the
beneficent planet, and to Hymen.

But alas,

> Al to litel, weylawey the whyle,
> Lasteth swich joye, ythonked be Fortune!

IV. 1–2

Venus begins to entertain the Furies in her mansion. At the beginning of the fifth and last book Criseyde is sent from Troy, and we are faced with the unrelieved pathos and sorrow of hope deferred, self-deceived, and at last miserably extinct. Troilus himself is 'despitously' slain by the fierce Achilles—but death is not a part of his tragedy, it is welcome to him, for he never ceases to love the faithless Criseyde. And here comes the surprise; 'Th'ende is every tales strengthe', as Pandarus and the proverbs say, and the rhetoricians taught. Chaucer takes us beyond death, and we see Troilus taken up into heaven, though the pagan colouring is maintained in the description. In heaven Troilus straightway despises earth in comparison with the joys he now experiences. He looks down to where he was slain,

> And in hymself he lough[1] right at the wo
> Of hem that wepten for his deth so faste;
> And dampned al oure werk[2] that foloweth so
> The blynde lust,[3] the which that may nat laste,
> And sholden al oure herte on heven caste.
>
> V. 1821–5

This passage was inserted in revision. It is not a mere afterthought; its function is to emphasize what immediately follows:

> Swich[4] fyn[5] hath, lo, this Troilus for love,
> Swich fyn hath al his grete worthinesse;
> Swich fyn hath his estat real[6] above,
> Swich fyn his lust, swich fyn hath his noblesse;
> Swich fyn hath false worldes brotelnesse,[7]
> And thus bigan his lovyng of Criseyde,
> As I have told, and in this wise he deyde.[8]

---

[1] laughed.   [2] misery, struggle.   [3] pleasure.   [4] such.
[5] end.   [6] royal.   [7] transitoriness.   [8] died.

O yonge, fresshe folkes, he or she,
In which that love up groweth with youre age,
Repeyreth[1] hom[2] fro worldly vanyte,
And of youre herte up casteth the visage
To thilke[3] God that after his ymage
Yow made, and thynketh al nys[4] but a faire
This world, that passeth soone as floures faire.

And loveth hym, the which that right for love
Upon a crois, oure soules for to beye,[5]
First starf,[6] and roos, and sit in hevene above;
For he nyl falsen no wight, dar I seye,
That wol his herte al holly on hym leye.
And syn[7] he best to love is, and most meke,
What nedeth feynede loves for to seke?

V. 1828–48

The poetry and passion of these stanzas are not less than those of the praise of Love. They are constant elements of Chaucer's thought. The whole situation is a parallel to that set forth in the *Parliament*, except that the *Parliament begins* with the despite of the world. We may even see the contrast in the *Parliament* between the lascivious Venus and Nature the 'vicar of God' set forth in the contrast between the lust of Diomede and the noble 'natural' love of Troilus. There is, however, some difference. First, Troilus's worst suffering has been due to Criseyde's 'untruth', secondly Troilus is dead. As to Criseyde's 'untruth'; it is contrasted with the everlasting Truth of Christ's love. Since we know that, why should we be miserable about the loss of 'feynede love'? This world is but a transitory fair—why should we take its transmutations too seriously? God grant us to take them for the best. This is a comment which arises *out of* the story; it is not so much a comment *on* the story. It is not a con-

[1] return.   [2] home   [3] that same.   [4] is not.   [5] buy.   [6] died.   [7] since.

demnation of Troilus, though had he followed this advice he would have been less miserable. Secondly, since this world is but transitory, death is inevitable, and does not matter. We may remember what Theseus says about the death of Arcite. Of course Troilus laughs at those mourning for him, for he has gone to a much better place than the world—'the pleyn felicitee of heaven'; why should they grieve for him? Such is the end of Troilus's love, his great worthiness, his royalty, his pleasure and his suffering—Heaven. It is only *when* he is in Heaven that he can see how trivial worldly suffering is. But if those in whom love is natural, the young, will only love Christ first, they will see before death how little they need worry about the ups-and-downs of life—though that does not mean that they will not have to endure them. The tension of the *Parliament* is thus to some extent resolved: the world is to be despised, but only from the point of view of Heaven. Contempt for it does not mean that it is out of God's rule. There is no 'repudiation of love' at the end of the *Troilus*; rather the point of view is shifted from the earthly plane to the heavenly. But Heaven and Earth are not utterly separate. The great chain of love extends from one to the other. However, the love between man and woman, though the greatest earthly good, is still *only* earthly. Chaucer does not make such love transcendental as Dante did. This is not surprising; 'For in the resurrection they neither marry nor are given in marriage, but are as the angels of God in heaven' (Matt. XXII, 30). Yet as far as earthly lovers are concerned, the mandate is equally strong. 'He which made them at the beginning made them male and female, and said "For this cause shall a man leave father and mother and shall cleave to his wife".' (Matt. XIX, 4–5.) Here the duality between earthly and heavenly is expressed in the source which Chaucer drew on more than any other, and which he must have accepted completely.

The *Troilus* ends with a prayer, which Chaucer in part borrows from Dante, where the sublimity of the Italian poet raises his great English reader and translator to a magnificence of speech, and a humble exaltation of spirit which he achieves nowhere else.

Chapter Eight

THE LEGEND OF GOOD WOMEN

THE years following 1386 were as usual troubled, and Chaucer himself perhaps in eclipse until 1389. The thin stream of references to him in the official documents continues. But their interpretation is often doubtful, and from none of them would it be gathered that he was a well-known court poet. Thomas Usk's reference to him as the 'noble philosophical poete' is worth the whole of them, establishing as it does a contemporary's estimate of his work, and the typical line of appreciation of the next two and a half centuries.

There are two main bodies of poetry filling Chaucer's later years, each composed of a Prologue introducing a collection of stories. The first of these is *The Legend of Good Women*, and the second, of course, *The Canterbury Tales*. The *Legend* is a pendant to the *Troilus*, yet in its form and its failure it provides a half-way house to the *Tales*. Its plan is simple to the point of boredom. The *Prologue* recounts a dream of the poet's, in which the god of love (a mythological figure to some extent of Chaucer's own creating) accuses Chaucer of holding it folly to serve love because he has published the untruth of Criseyde, thereby casting a general aspersion on women's constancy, and has translated the 'heretical' *Roman de la Rose*. The god's consort, Queen Alceste, endeavours to soften the charge, while recounting Chaucer's other works in praise of love. She mentions such 'other holyness' as his translation of Boethius, his life of Saint Cecilia, and another work, now lost. To include such 'holiness', as he also calls these works in the *Retraccioun* condemning his secular works, is a queer inconsistency, but perhaps Chaucer was taking a useful opportunity to list, and, so to speak, to 'sign' some of his major works, as he does in the Prologue to the *Man of Law's Tale* and even in his *Retraccioun*. At all events, Chaucer denies the god's accusation, and Chaucer is right—he is no heretic to love, no defamer of women. But nevertheless he has to pay the penalty, which is to write a glorious 'legend' (i.e. a Saint's Tale) of women true in love. This he undertakes to do, although the god of love says there are so many of them that he will only be able to make a short tale of each. Nine of these tales follow, but the series is unfinished.

Each of the tales has, in effect, the same theme as the *Troilus* (for the *Troilus* is a story of true love) and is essentially a counterpart to the *Troilus*, although so much poorer in poetry. The tales certainly are not a repudiation of the so-called repudiation of love at the end of the *Troilus*. They are written to assert the trueness of women against what is said to be Chaucer's imputation of their falseness. The *Legends* are remarkable for their thinness when compared with Chaucer's other treatments of closely similar themes. Perhaps Chaucer, without immediately realizing it, had written himself out on this aspect of love in the *Troilus*. Another reason, doubtless, was that there seemed so many stories to be told that each was rather cramped. Like the later project of one hundred and twenty Canterbury Tales, it was too ambitious a scheme, and had the further disastrous disadvantage of a single monotonous theme. Chaucer may have learnt from this failure the need for that dramatic variety so apparent in the *Tales*.

Yet the *Legends* are worth the connoisseur's attention. There are some fine descriptions, like Dido's lively hunt and Cleopatra's sea-battle. There are noble and touching speeches. But the poems are chiefly interesting because in them Chaucer is attempting, not always successfully or patiently, that art of rapid plain narration of which Gower was the greater master. In the *Legends* the situation and the sentiments are all. The set task required repetition, and Chaucer wearied towards the end, as we do, of the lack of variety. Nevertheless, within the narrow limits there is considerable diversity, and the tales of Dido, Ariadne, Pyramus and Thisbe, and especially Lucrece, are masterpieces of this, for Chaucer, unusually swift plain art. They are 'line-drawings'—not oil-paintings—of beautiful sad virtue, revealing at times a severe rationalism, a dry medieval contempt for pagan heroes and vices. To look for deep feelings, detailed characterisation, much splendid or realistic description, is to seek what could not be there. And though Chaucer at times expresses unseemly haste we should not exaggerate into a pervading comic irony either such expressions or those others where, in some of the tales, Chaucer again shows the strain and breaks decorum with forced rhetoric or a natural flippancy.

The *Prologue* to the *Legends* is something much more familiar and typically varied, presenting its old and conventional devices with a fresh immediacy. The fourteenth-century preciosity of daisy-worship astonishingly accommodates cynical jokes, lyrical description, personal defence. The *Prologue* is also, however, unique in showing Chaucer revising his own work, and discussion of this special interest must take priority. The earlier version called BF, was probably written in 1386, and revised about 1395, giving us AG.

The structure of BF is rambling, and there is an awkward confusion between Alceste and 'my lady' (cf. 249 ff., 432, and 540). AG does a certain amount of tidying up and the confusion about Alceste is removed. In BF the subject of the fashionable controversy between the Flower and the Leaf[1] is approached in 72, but is not actually developed until 188–96. In AG these two references are consolidated in 65–78. Again, in AG the dream starts earlier. The effect of this alteration is to put that famous description of the beautiful morning and the charmingly anthropomorphic behaviour of the birds *inside* the dream. This brings AG more into line with the construction of the beginning of the *Roman*, and is an improvement. The morning, for all its freshness, is nothing like the chilly hours just following dawn of an ordinary English May morning. It has the warmth and sweetness of a kindlier clime. It is in fact very much in the French literary tradition, and is much easier to accept as part of the Dream; it is more sensible, and therefore more poetic. The general effect of this and other structural changes is to consolidate, to make the development less wandering and casual.

AG also develops certain matters more lightly touched on in BF. In the earlier version Chaucer says that a king's subjects 'are his treasure and his gold in coffer'—a very appropriate sentiment for a customs officer. In the later version he cuts out this not very good line and inserts six lines about the duty of a king to hear his subjects' complaints and petitions. Whenever Chaucer approaches political themes in later life he is always earnest and

---

[1] It is very characteristic of Chaucer that he says that he himself is on neither side. The Flower seems to have been favoured by the Lancastrians.

orthodox. Nevertheless, in AG the central occasion of the Prologue seems to be taken less seriously. There can be little doubt that Chaucer, by this time not very active at Court, was revising simply from a literary point of view. He could not refrain from a little mocking with a solemn face. In the long and important insertion, AG 258–312, he gives the god of love a much livelier and fuller speech. The god accuses Chaucer of heresy against him, although Chaucer owns a lot of books telling the lives of women, 'and ever a hundred good against one bad':

> What seith Valerye, Titus or Claudian?
> What seith Jerome agayns Jovynyan?

What Jerome said against Jovinian is touched on in the Wife of Bath's Prologue. He and 'Valerian' (i.e. Walter Map) were perhaps the most satirical and effective of all the many slanderers of women in the anti-feminist Middle Ages. Chaucer loved them as much as he loved the tales of noble women. Here he is deliberately making a fool of the god of love. This may reflect his increasing years, but it is not the first time he has imperilled the general unity of a poem for the sake of a joke. He makes other ironical additions. The Queen defends him by suggesting that he translated poems, and 'knew not what he was saying'. On the other hand he cut out BF 152, which is no better than a rather feeble leer about sexual functions.

Most of the alterations are obviously aimed to improve the sense and the poetry. Thus he cut out the last twenty-five lines of BF. They are somewhat verbose, and are little loss. At the beginning he much modified the expression of his love for the daisy. It is difficult not to sense some personal feeling in the early, BF, version of this—perhaps it was a courtier's address to the Queen.

I

Chaucer may have modified it later because the Queen's
death made it inappropriate, or even simply because the
daisy-cult was no longer a fashion in sentiment which
appealed to him. Some of the alterations at the beginning
forced him to abandon the charming four-line song which
in BF introduced Alceste's attendants. Chaucer's will-
ingness to abandon these excellent few lines in the interests of the whole is a mark of his maturity and self-
confidence as craftsman and artist. Other changes are
often minute, but hardly less interesting. Thus he tones
down the rather mechanical emphasis on the brightness
of the God of Love. For 'holiness' (BF 424) he substitutes 'busy-ness' (AG 412). Where BF 348–9 describes
Love as a god who knows all, AG 323–7 substitutes the
remark that all is not true which the god of love hears.
Occasionally the alteration merely cuts out the clumsy
repetition of the same word, e.g. the repetition of
'serve' in BF 326–7. The later version also writes at
somewhat greater length of Geoffrey Chaucer himself, in
the familiar image (which seems to have assuaged both his
modesty and that desire to introduce himself into his
poetry which he shares with Langland and Gower), of an
amiable but absurd simpleton.

In general, the revision gives a stronger sense of the
poet's personality, a better construction with some ex-
travagances pruned, and a strengthened style. The AG
version is livelier in humour, and also warmer in its
praises of noble women. Against these advantages must
be set a slight loss of spontaneity and freedom from care,
and also some flaws in the underlying unity of mood; for
parts of AG are more serious, other parts more flippant,
than in the earlier version. Nevertheless, for all the
tinkering, it is still the same poem. The wonderfully
fresh sense of spring remains, with the poet's heart-

warming confession of inability to read in the stirring time of the year. There is still the delight in books, together with a little more information on the books Chaucer has read or written.

Being so much older when he revises, Chaucer is at once more serious and less solemn. He takes his mythology and his courtly fashions more lightly. He has acquired a more level tone, and a greater control over his materials. He appears altogether more self-assured.

Perhaps between the two versions of the Prologue Chaucer's interests turned away from the courtly subject of love and of the fundamental problems raised by love. He may have felt he had worked that vein. It is also a matter of common experience that as a man grows older he becomes less interested in fundamental questions, for willy-nilly he has made up his mind about them. Interest tends to turn from philosophy to ethics; from theories to facts. We may perceive this happening even in the difference between the *Parliament* and the *Troilus*. The *Canterbury Tales* are evidence of the continuation of the process.

Many critics have sought an allegorical significance in the figures of Queen Alceste and the god of love. Some have seen in Alceste an allegory of Queen Anne. But since Alceste tells the poet to present his poem to the Queen at Eltham or Sheen, Alceste and Queen Anne can hardly be equated. Nor would Chaucer have treated the god of love so flippantly if he were intended to represent King Richard. The idea that Alceste represents a great patroness of Chaucer's is more feasible; but decisive evidence is lacking. In view of the mention of Alceste at the end of the *Troilus* and the entirely self-explanatory nature of the Prologue, there seems no need to suppose any allegorical significance.

Before coming to the *Canterbury Tales* we may take this opportunity of noticing the *Treatise on the Astrolabe*, written for Chaucer's little son Lewis, probably about 1392. It is an elementary treatise, mainly translated, on the principal instrument used by astronomers in observing the stars. It is pleasant to see Chaucer, at the height of his powers, engaged with all seriousness and effort on this task for his son, although he never finished it. Perhaps there was a pedagogic vein in Chaucer as in Milton. One suspects, too, that like the later poet he may have somewhat overestimated his pupil's capacity for instruction. Chaucer does not set himself up as a practising scientist: 'I n'am but a lewd compilator of the labour of olde astrologiens, and have it translatyd in myn Englissh oonly for thy doctrine. And with this swerd shal I sleen envie.' The work is of some interest for historians of early science and of English prose.

A discovery has recently been made by Dr. Derek Price of Cambridge, which may be exciting. This is another scientific treatise of about the same date, called the *Equatorie of the Planetis*. Dr. Price thinks that this may not only be by Chaucer, but the very manuscript may be written in his own hand. Apart from the strong sentimental interest of having a piece of Chaucer's own writing, we can expect, if it is indeed proved to be Chaucer's, to have a great deal of valuable information about his spelling and handwriting which should greatly affect editors' treatment of his texts. Until now, no piece of his writing, save signatures, has been known. The manuscript may afford other information, but it is too early as yet to say.

Chapter Nine

PROLOGUE TO THE CANTERBURY TALES

The Canterbury Tales have always been by far the most popular of Chaucer's works. There are some eighty-four full manuscripts or fragments and six early printed editions, compared with twenty manuscripts and three early printed editions of the *Troilus*. The reason is not far to seek: the *Troilus* is long, serious, learned and magnificent; the *Tales* are short, varied, and often humorous. The *Troilus* is more often mentioned in early records because literary criticism until Dryden tended to be technical and didactic, in a word, 'highbrow'. The ordinary reader has always been more easily captivated by the *Tales*. Their demands are less uncompromising, they contain some of Chaucer's best work, and they offer more opportunities for skipping. There is something for everyone in them, and their richness is inexhaustible.

It is the greater pity that the work was not only unfinished, but left in a state of very great confusion. Gaps between the stories and inconsistencies in their order abound. It is obvious, too, that several tales were due for a revision which they never received. Chaucer's use of stories written by him before he thought of the pilgrimage to Canterbury, and his own changes of mind in conducting the general scheme, have added to the difficulties. While it is impossible here to do more than touch on the problems which exist, a reference to Chaucer's methods of composition and publishing will at once suggest the difficulties and improve our understanding of his poetic aims.

We have none of his 'foul papers', which may have been lightly waxed tablets, but his working copies of poems would have been loose sheets of paper or vellum which he bound up in booklets of at most a few stories at a time. When satisfied with what he wrote, he sent it off to a professional scribe to have one or more copies written out fair. Scribes were liable to make many mistakes, so Chaucer corrected the copy when it came back (scratching mistakes out with stone or a knife), cursing the scribe meanwhile. Much of this we know from the short poem which is the unenviable monument of his usual scribe.

> Adam scriveyn, if ever it thee bifalle
> Boece or Troylus for to wryten newe,
> Under thy long lokkes thou most have the scalle,[1]
> But[2] after[3] my makyng thou wryte more trewe;
> So ofte a-daye I mot[4] thy werk renewe,
> It to correcte and eek to rubbe and scrape;
> And al is thorugh thy negligence and rape.[5]

Chaucer published a poem in two ways; either by reading it aloud or by allowing copies to circulate. The famous *Troilus* 'frontispiece' depicts Chaucer himself reading to the Court. However, the 'frontispiece' is by no means realistic and was painted after Chaucer's death; and it is curious that there seems to be no other reference to the reading of longish poems in a court except Froissart's account of reading his own *Meliador* at the court of Gaston de Foix. Perhaps the more usual situation was similar to Criseyde's 'reading-party', where a book is read to a small group of friends. The Court at large

[1] scab.   [2] unless.   [3] according to.   [4] must.   [5] haste.

seems to have been fonder of music and songs. Most people heard literature; a few, mainly those in the learned professions, read. Even when manuscripts were lent out and copied, there would be many who heard for one who read. A manuscript was read until it fell to pieces. It was also copied, by amateurs and professionals. A bad copy might be made of a manuscript which had already lost several pages and was itself a bad copy of another. Copyists made every conceivable error—missing out letters, words, pages; misunderstanding, miswriting; often they wrote in different dialects; sometimes they altered passages which for some reason seemed wrong to them, or of which they disapproved. Chaucer himself complicated the situation when, as we know happened with the *Troilus* and the Prologue to the *Legends*, he continued to revise the poem after copies had been made for circulation. When two or three versions of a poem thus existed, it sometimes happened that a copyist combined fragments from different states of the poem to make one whole; or 'corrected' one copy by reference to another representing a different state of revision; thus contamination arises. When, as happened with the *Tales*, the author continually alters the work piecemeal, and perhaps never issues it whole in his lifetime, the state of the manuscripts is chaotic. There are many inconsistencies which we may guess Chaucer would not have noticed, or bothered about, but many others which he would have removed on full revision. Even worse, it is not the originally confused manuscripts which have descended to us, but their descendants through the hands of an unknown number of copyists, many of whom made their own attempts to sort out the muddle—sometimes even by adding their own verses. It is not necessarily the best manuscripts, either, which have survived the accidents of flood, fire, children, vandals, and other enemies of books, including those who love them so much that they read them to pieces.[1] A good deal of disagreement exists as to the date of writing the various stories. But by this time, variety not development is the mark of Chaucer's genius. Approaching the sea of eternity he spreads himself like a river-delta. It is the same river everywhere, the same elements are present, but in a multitude of different courses, each channel smaller than the earlier main stream, though the magnitude and diversity of the total are greater. This short essay cannot explore each separate creek, delightful as that would be.

It is not known when Chaucer first thought of the idea of the *Canterbury Tales*. Professor Carleton Browne suggested that he began to write them as early as 1384, in that most fruitful period at the Customs House. More orthodox opinion usually says about 1387, when Chaucer was living down in Kent. There were several well-known collections of stories held together by some single idea, or placed in a single framework. Gower was in process of writing such a collection, and Chaucer's own *Legends* are another example. The short story was the most characteristic form of fourteenth-century literature. It conveyed all kinds of literary effects. An audience, as opposed to a reader, can better understand and remember a story than any other form of literary expres-

[1] The labour of scholars has to some extent prepared a path for the general reader through the wilderness. The stories fall into certain well-defined groups. Skeat represents those scholars who, by reference to internal evidence, place the groups in order according to details of the journey, labelling them from A to I. Robinson and Manly represent more modern editors who deny themselves this reconstruction, since it is not represented in any manuscript, and accept the somewhat arbitrary and slightly different order of the best manuscript, the Ellesmere. They number the groups from one to ten, splitting Skeat's group B into B^1 (Fragment II) and B^2 (Fragment VII). Both methods of annotation will be used here, and Skeat's order followed.

sion. For the more sophisticated, a story could be analysed, and there might be as many as three or four different levels on which a story might be understood. Most stories, however, were simply anecdotes on one level, and of these a great number were current of all kinds, pious, amusing, improper. Most of these were never written down, although some of them, as habits of reading and writing spread, tended to be caught up by literary men. Apart from what he might hear Chaucer also read many stories and we may well understand the attraction they had for him, both as a typical man of his times, and as a literary artist seeking satisfactory forms. We can also see that there would be two types of raw material ready to his hand—stories written down in earlier authors; and current tales. In general it was the more serious stories which had been written down, the lighter ones told. Often a story was believed to be historical and therefore true simply because it was written down. The *Clerk's Tale* of patient Griselda is the subject of two illuminating comments in this respect, quoted by Professor Manly. One of Petrarch's friends doubted whether the story could be true. Petrarch replied that such stories as those of Alcestis (who went to the Underworld in place of her husband, and was rescued by Hercules) *seem* to be fables (fabulas)—'Atque historiae verae sunt', 'but they are true histories'. The sensible fifteenth-century citizen who wrote the *Menagier de Paris* also tells the story of Griselda, and says, 'I do not believe it ever happened, but the story is such that I dare not correct or change it, for one wiser than I compiled it, and gave it its name'. There was therefore a clear difference between a 'fabula' and a 'historia'. And whereas the plot itself could not be altered, a great part of the aim of such rhetoricians as Geoffroi de Vinsauf was to teach how to dress up an old story in a new signification. It was also taught that style should suit subject-matter—high subject, high style. 'Low' subjects, therefore, which dealt with humble people and trivial or amusing events, were not to be dressed in the panoply of high style, unless the poet's aim was burlesque.

The quality of Chaucer's genius and originality is especially clear in the use he made of the raw material and the ideas which he shared with Gower and Boccaccio. It was natural in that age to attempt to gather in every kind of story, to put the serious subject by the amusing, the parody of the high style not far from the high style itself, the 'pious fable' by the 'dirty story'—in a word, to sum up as much of human experience as possible, to let 'contraries meet in one'. Even in Boccaccio's *Decameron* there are plenty of serious and pious tales. Chaucer goes further than his contemporaries, however, in his variety; and especially in accounting for it by the characters of those who tell the tales. We may guess that his characters were first the product, so to speak, of the tales they were to tell. It is certain that Chaucer had some stories by him that were already written before the *Tales* as a whole were conceived. He may have wished to use these up, and to provide a series of pegs on which to hang the many more stories he wished to write. Perhaps he wrote the General Prologue to the *Canterbury Tales* at this stage of his idea. However that may be, the characters once conceived took on almost a life of their own, and the whole scheme continued to develop under his careful fostering and pruning. We can see a good idea succeeded by a better, for example, when he substituted the present *Wife of Bath's Tale* for the tale originally given to her which is now called the *Shipman's Tale*. The change is apparent because the present *Shipman's Tale*, although unquestionably his according to the manuscripts, is in fact written for a woman to tell. It belongs to the period of the *Tales*, and could only fit the Wife of Bath. Here is a case where the speed of development outpaced Chaucer; he had no time to complete the other half of his plan, and alter the wording of the *Shipman's Tale* to make it accord with the speaker. From similar inconsistencies in the text it is usually assumed that the prose *Tale of Melibeus* was first assigned to the Man of Law, and then later switched to its position as Chaucer's own second tale, perhaps to add its weight of contrast to the brilliant sequence of Fragment VII (B2). When this was done, the Man of Law was given his present tale of *Constance*. The developments of the plan involving a change of attribution of the stories went hand in hand with Chaucer's writing of the Links between the tales. These are no mere connections. They have been called the finest tale of all, for the characters which in the General Prologue are somewhat static, for all their brilliance, talk among themselves on the road between stories—and when people begin to *talk* in Chaucer we hear the very tones of living voices. The coarser characters quarrel, Miller against Reeve, Friar against Summoner. One tells a story against the other, churls tell churls' tales. Who shall say here which came first— such stories as make a pair and give rise to characters, or characters who quarrel, giving rise to stories in which they attack each other? We may as well ask which came first, the chicken or the egg. Nevertheless, in at least one case, the character came first; this is the Wife of Bath, for since she was presumably first meant to tell the *Shipman's Tale*, her present tale may be thought of as particularly hers. Even so, it is not so much the product of her character as, say, one of Hamlet's soliloquies is a

product of his. Her tale of Gawayn is a fairy-tale, a
wonder, told in a mood of delicate fantasy (though the
plot was not of course invented by Chaucer). Now delicacy is not one of the Wife of Bath's characteristics. To
understand and enjoy the story and its placing to the full
the tale's reflections on sovereignty in marriage should
be compared with the similar reflections—how differently expressed—in the Wife's own lengthy Prologue
to her tale. There is a most delightful contrast between
her own comic and lusty coarseness (itself a satire upon
her whole argument) and the charm of her Tale. In the
succession of Tales which follows hers (Fragments III,
IV, V, Groups DEF) the theme of marriage relationships
is raised fairly frequently, though the sequence is hardly
to be regarded as a debate on marriage, as some imply.
But it is convenient to retain the name of the Marriage
Group for these three Fragments, and we shall miss some
of the significance of the *Wife of Bath's Tale* if we do not
recognize its contribution to the theme of marriage.
Only a small part of its significance lies in its expression of
character.

From this brief survey, it is clear that the essential
quality of the *Canterbury Tales* as a whole lies in the inter-
play of stories, rather than in the interaction of the
characters who tell the stories. The method may be
compared with that of a painter who plans the areas of
colour on his picture, some passages to support each
other, some to contrast. Just as Chaucer seems to have
planned the *Parliament*, balancing and contrasting Nature
with the lascivious Venus, and the *Somnium Scipionis* with
both, so he seems to have planned his *Tales*, though he
got no further than Fragments. Or in other words, the
sequence of stories is similar to the events of a plot, and
the characters are motivated so as to make their actions

(i.e. their stories) seem suitable. By so regarding the *Tales* we may appreciate such of their total design as Chaucer lived to finish. On occasion the demands of the pattern of stories cause minor inconsistencies of character, as when that fashionable and self-confident huntsman, the Monk of the Prologue, tells his string of bookish and sententious Tragedies. Chaucer needed someone to relate them, and the Monk, though not a perfect candidate, was because of his profession the most suitable of the Pilgrims. In many cases the story told is neither particularly suited nor unsuited to the teller. We also find that within a given tale the conception of the character who is supposed to be telling it is now strong, now weak. Chaucer often seems to speak in a tale of his own person.

Such trivial inconsistencies hardly amount to a fault. But they remind us that the realism of the *Tales* is superficial and not to be taken too seriously. It is silly to speculate whether Chaucer may be recording an actual pilgrimage, nor need we expect him to display characters in action like a modern novelist. It is also doubtful whether we can draw any valid conclusions about the chronological developments of his scheme from variations in the presentation of a character at different parts of the work.

But whenever Chaucer sets a group of people talking, especially from the middle or lower classes, where he can indulge a satirical humour without the need to convey the 'high sentence' of his aristocratic ideal, their arguments ding in our ears, the breath they breathe is the common air, flavoured, it may well be, with malt. We notice the same thing in the *Parliament* where the raucous comic voices of duck and goose live in our memory long after those of the 'gentil' (i.e. noble) falcons have faded to silence. Chaucer's most memorable characters and speeches are probably not those to which he himself attached most importance. In this respect he a little resembles that other gentlemanly writer, Sir Walter Scott, whose low-life dialogue is so vastly superior to that of his well-bred heroes and heroines.

We do not only hear the Pilgrims, we see them before us in their very habits as they lived, for Chaucer with the apparent simplicity of truly original genius paints their portraits in the General Prologue before he sets them on their way to Canterbury. For all its simplicity there seems to be nothing in European literature like it, before or since.

The General Prologue opens with a passage about Spring of the kind no writer could omit. Boccaccio has one in his Latin handbook of mythology, Creton in his French chronicle of Richard's deposition, and there are many others. So familiar a subject could surprise no audience. The triumph of the opening as literary art lies in its purposive structure and its style. This elaborate introduction takes less than twenty lines, and in it we have smelt the spring air, and have swooped in imagination down from the Zodiac to the Tabard. The focus has carried us from a general view of the season to fix sharply on the nine-and-twenty pilgrims gathered in a well-known inn near London. The vision is both spacious and precise. The passage is written in a modified 'high style'. The first two lines are simple and direct, so that no listener or reader can miss the point. The next three lines, with their almost scientifically elaborate mention of the nourishing of plants, are written in that poetic diction for which Chaucer was so venerated in the following two centuries; he calls water, *licour*, the west wind *Zephirus*. The third line shows Chaucer's magic fully at work, with the image of Zephirus in the first

half, and the realistic 'sweet breath' in the second. The
fanciful personification of the west wind gives him not
only a colourful and musical word in itself—it presses
home the sensuous realism of 'sweet breath'. There is
the same splendour and simplicity in the next two lines,
and by this time he can well afford one of his favourite
astronomical references to the date—it heightens the
style, and cannot be misunderstood. He continues with
a line of the most striking simplicity and musical beauty:

> And smalé fowelés maken melodyé.

The commonplace reference to the song of birds in
spring becomes beautiful and arresting partly from the
music of the line, and partly from its position in the
poetic unit, which is the paragraph. Chaucer's poetic
power is only rarely distilled in a word or a phrase; it is
to be sought in the paragraph and even larger units.
Narrative poetry, especially when written partly for an
audience, is as a rule diffuse and repetitive. It is to be
taken in large draughts, not sipped; a table-wine, not a
liqueur. But here, in this rhetorical and superbly poetic
beginning to his poem, Chaucer gives us the delights of
both narrative and lyric.

The portraits of the Prologue have the same concentrated brilliance. Chaucer describes a man as if his eye
were wandering over him, noticing a bright detail
here and there, which he equally haphazardly records.
There seems nothing more natural in the world, but this
very impression of casualness, this economy, significance
and variety of detail clearly tell of that supreme art which
conceals art. There is no pattern of description. Sometimes the visible details of dress come first, and through
them we see the character. The Knight's gipoun is still
marked by the rust and oil from his armour, and his

horses are good. Mere factual information, it seems; yet
from these we learn that he has wasted no time after his
safe return home to go on his pilgrimage. He is not concerned with a smart outward appearance, but he is not
poor, nor neglectful of his essential equipment as can be
seen from his horses. Sometimes Chaucer describes a
person's character, and adds almost as an afterthought
those details of dress which set him vividly before our
eyes and reinforce what is already known of him. There
is a different method for almost every pilgrim. The
sketches are very brief, yet by including snatches of conversation, and by describing in many cases the opinions,
usual activities, or dwelling place of a person, Chaucer
conveys a strong sense of individuality, and depth of
portraiture. The necessary shortness of the description
leads Chaucer to lay detail close by detail, often in a non-
logical order. The impression of naivety which this com-
pression sometimes gives may be compared with Chaucer's
fondness for portraying himself in his own poetry as a
foolish simple man. The sugar-coating of naivety contrasts
pleasantly with the sharpness of wit it pretends to con-
ceal. Thus of the Cook Chaucer says:

> But greet harm was it, as it thoughte[1] me
> That on his shyne[2] a mormal[3] hadde he.
> For blankmanger,[4] that made he with the beste.
>
> I (A), 385-7

The poetry is in the piquancy.

Not all the characters are treated ironically. There is
variety of mood. All the pilgrims are presented in terms
of their occupations (this is partly the secret of their
astonishing variety). Then, there is an element of ideali-
zation in the actual description of characters; almost

[1] seemed to.   [2] shin.   [3] running sore.   [4] white food (creamed fowl, etc.).

every person, whether good or bad, is said to be the perfect example of his or her kind. The faint exaggeration
sharpens the outlines of the sketches. Chaucer exagger-
ates both good and bad, but the distortion is more
noticeable in the case of good characters, and the
characters he satirizes are livelier than those he respects.
It is easy to see that like Langland he venerates the medieval ideal of the three basic orders of society, Knighthood,
Clergy, Ploughmen: Ploughmen to work with their hands
and gain food for all; Clergy to foster and protect the
souls of all; Knighthood to maintain justice and protect
the lives and property of all. Chaucer does not satirize
those Pilgrims who represent this ideal of society. Thus
although details of the Knight's career can be paralleled
in the lives of contemporaries, the total impression of
his character is very different from our impression of the
usual fourteenth-century representative of his Order.
Even when all allowances have been made for the ease
with which we detect the beams in the eyes of our fore-
fathers, it is obvious that the Knight is an idealized portrait. That does not make him any the less pleasant and
inspiring to read about, loving as he does, 'Trouthe and
honour, fredom (i.e. generosity of spirit) and curtesie';
he has fought for our faith against the pagan, a lion in the
field, a lamb in hall. With him goes the Squire, youthful,
romantic, courtly, in whom love upgroweth with his age,
but who when the time of young love is passed, we may
well suppose will take on the sterner duties of knighthood. Clergy is represented partly by the Clerk, who
speaks for the life of learning. These three portraits are
entirely convincing, for Chaucer was writing well within
the range of his own experience and personal ideals. The
other representative of Clergy is the Parson, in whom is
seen the humility and holiness, the active well-doing,

praying and preaching, enjoined upon priests. The
Ploughman, brother to the Parson, represents the third
order of the ideal medieval society. The Parson, and
especially the Ploughman, are the most idealized of all
the Pilgrims, and the least vividly portrayed. They are
theories rather than persons. Their poetic force comes
from the beauty of the ideal itself, and Chaucer's too
rarely acknowledged power of writing idealistic poetry.

The three orders of society, and the system of Christian
ethics implied by them, are, by a paradox, the perfectly
serious frame to Chaucer's so famous 'comic view of
life'. In other words, nearly every pilgrim when judged
according to this exacting ideal, inevitably appears ridiculous or self-seeking or wicked, or all of these. Thus
Chaucer does not much care for the new classes, the
nouveau-riche land-acquiring Lawyer, the usurious Merchant with his shady exchange practices. He makes the
orthodox jokes about Doctors—their study is but little
on the Bible, and they make money out of the sick and
suffering. His treatment of the religious orders, all of
whom should have accorded with the ideal of Clergy,
varies with the individual. The Prioress, with her gentle-
ness, her social pretensions, her minor but constant
evasions of her Rule in favour of a ladylike worldliness,
is presented with a mild and amused irony. The able,
vigorous, luxurious Monk with all the tastes of an
eighteenth-century country gentlemen, is both appreciated and mocked:

> What[1] sholde he studie and make hymselven wood[2]
> Upon a book in cloystre alwey to poure,
> Or swynken[3] with his handes, and laboure,
> As Austyn[4] bit?[5] How shal the world be served?
>
>   I (A), 184–7

[1] why.   [2] mad.   [3] toil.   [4] St. Augustine.   [5] bade.

It is from the world's point of view that Chaucer remarks, in his innocent way,

> And I seyde his opinion was good.
>
> I (A), 183

Never mind that the world is little and contemptible and must pass away, while Heaven endures for ever. The Friar and Summoner (very unpopular members of society) are satirized increasingly strongly, while the Pardoner is mercilessly exposed for a lying, fraudulent, grasping, conceited eunuch.

Langland with the same ideals describes the same state of society and some of the same types with a desperate zeal for reform, a passion of pity and condemnation, but above all with a spiritual vision which in one flight at least puts him among the very few English poets even to challenge Dante on anything like his own ground. Chaucer is an interesting contrast. For all his intelligence and piety he has no spiritual vision, here or elsewhere. He never seems angry, and rarely condemns. He is no zealous reformer; he has neither the faith nor the optimism for that; he has too subtle a mind, is too convinced of the badness of the world. He maintains a well-bred, courtly, imperturbable front which nothing can shock. In the General Prologue he is a descriptive poet, with convictions indeed, but also with a connoisseur's appreciation of types. Here, he seems to say, is something very fine of its kind. He can enjoy without necessarily liking. He can laugh without feeling affection, accept without approving.[1]

[1] The sense of humour has probably undergone some historical change. Although no one likes being laughed at, it seems to be generally assumed by modern critics that if we laugh at a person or a character in literature, we have some degree of kindly feeling towards him. In our earlier literature laughter and scorn are very closely allied. Sir Philip Sidney, in the *Apologie for poetrie*, says, 'laughter hath onely a scornful tickling'.

It is not very likely, however, that Chaucer *consciously* constructed the social and ethical framework of the General Prologue. The framework is there because it was part of Chaucer's mind; it was his mode of looking at people, and he wrote about them as he saw them. No one can feel he is describing marionettes. Moreover, it has long been known that at least one of his characters had a counterpart in real life; Harry Bailly, innkeeper of Southwark, Host to the pilgrims, actually existed. He must have been a person well known in a London of only 45,000 inhabitants. He was twice Member of Parliament, and often acted as tax-collector, coroner, etc., as well as being an innkeeper on the much-frequented London-Canterbury-Dover road. Whether he was as Chaucer describes him we shall probably never know. The Merchant may possibly be meant to suggest a well-known merchant and money-lender named Gilbert Maghfeld, from whom Chaucer and several other courtiers are known to have borrowed money. Again, the Man of Law may have been meant to call to mind the distinguished Serjeant-at-law Thomas Pynchbeck, on the opposite side, politically, to Chaucer. He had offended Chaucer's friend Sir William Beauchamp, and had once signed a writ to arrest Chaucer for a small debt. Other identifications rather less certain have been proposed for others of the pilgrims. None of this affects their literary value now, but it seems certain that at least some of the satirical descriptions are meant to be hits at individuals who were well known to Chaucer and his immediate circle, while the portrait of the innkeeper made the whole account more entertaining and realistic. There are private jokes which we shall never share. The situation may be similar to that of some of Pope's personal satires, where one individual is principally aimed at, but through him a whole class or general type as well. Both the inner circle of readers and the general public are thereby pleased.

For all the variety of attitude in this extraordinarily rich Prologue, comic satire predominates. There are, therefore, certain limitations of scope. The higher aristocracy are excluded, for the Knight is comparatively low-ranking, and is in any case an ideal figure. The painfulness and rough comedy of the life of the great mass of the really poor find no place, and again their two representatives are idealized portraits. The characters of highest and lowest were not suitable for comic treatment, while in any case Chaucer seems to have had relatively little intimate knowledge of the poor, as we at once realize when we compare him with Langland. In the Prologue we mainly see the middling people, and we see them through Chaucer's eyes from a slightly superior moral and social station. We can afford to laugh at them. We look through the eyes of a poet masculine, self-assured, delighted, who knows there is 'joy after woe, and after joy, sadness' but is not at the moment concerned to point it out. He sees abuses but is neither surprised nor stung by them—after all what else can we expect from the world? And is there not a providential order? As several characters in his stories say, God makes nothing in vain. Men are not angels, but neither are they devils. Chaucer gives us a vision of men and women in the world, and most of them have some relish of absurdity when looked at carefully—especially when they require neither our loyalty nor our fear.

Chapter Ten

THE CANTERBURY TALES

THE Host's good wine and cheerful enthusiasm easily persuade the pilgrims, some thirty in number, to give their oath to tell two stories each on the way to Canterbury, and two on the way back. The tales that shall 'shorten their way' must be either instructive or amusing, either of 'sentence' or 'solas'. In an age unsated by newspaper and radio mere information was rated much higher than now, and stories of downright moral instruction in particular seem to have been relished by Chaucer and his audience as much as amusing anecdotes. His dramatic audience is the group of pilgrims; his real audience was composed of the members of the court, of important city merchants, of such clerics as the 'courtier bishops', and of such fellow writers as Hoccleve, a clerk in the Chancery offices, the poet and lawyer Ralph Strode, the poet and small landowner Gower.

To begin the *Tales* Chaucer fires off his heaviest broadside, the *Knight's Tale*. This tale of 'high sentence', written some years before, was now adapted to begin the series. It has already been discussed (Chapter VII) and no more need be done here than to agree with young and old among the Pilgrims, and especially with the 'gentils', that it is a noble story. It seems likely, however, that the Miller has been occupying his time otherwise than by listening, for he is by now very, very drunk. Not even the Host, by command or entreaty, can control him, and he insists on his 'churl's tale'. Chaucer apologizes, but pleads the duty of *exact* reporting: he has not invented the tale. If you do not wish to hear it, you may turn the page, there are plenty of 'storial' things, concerning nobility, morality, and also holiness. So Chaucer neatly puts the onus for any shock to the feelings upon reader rather than writer. (Perhaps he had readers more than hearers in mind in this last great work.)

The contrast between the *Miller's Tale* and the *Knight's Tale* is very refreshing, and very typical of Chaucer. We turn from 'sentence' to 'solas', from art in the service of serious conviction to art in the service of fun. The plot of the *Miller's Tale* is as fantastic as that of any romance, but Chaucer as usual brings the characters to life and makes the setting realistic. The difference from, say, the *Troilus* is that 'matter' or plot, and presentation are at one, and that there is not even any mock 'sentence' —men shall not make earnest of game. The plot is a common folk-tale, but none of the analogues in any way rival Chaucer's telling of the tale. There is for example a kind of poetry of absurdity in the way the carpenter is taken in by the tale of the tub. Some of the analogues miss this out completely; others attempt the impossible task of making the trick itself seem reasonable; Chaucer creates his carpenter the very kind of man to believe such nonsense. It is partly the unrestrained comic absurdity of the basic plot which helps to make the tale innocuous. The story is not related merely to make an opportunity for talking about adultery; the adultery is the end, but the joke is in the means to the end, and Chaucer concentrates on the joke, though he does not forget the end.

It is also extremely interesting to see what Chaucer puts in and what he leaves out. The physical realism, the 'visibility' of characters and setting was never more brilliantly conveyed.

> Imagination bodies forth
> The forms of things unknown, the poet's pen
> Turns them to shapes, and gives to airy nothing
> A local habitation and a name.

Of no poet is this truer than the comic poet. This is an elementary principle, and thus the Flemish analogue of the *Miller's Tale* is set in Antwerp, the Italian in Naples, and the *Miller's Tale* itself in Osney near Oxford, a place well known to many of his audience. The very house can almost be measured—the height of the window from the ground (an important point), the hole in the door of Nicholas's room big enough for a cat to pass through. We are conscious of the whole life of the village, as we see Absolon about his business and pleasure or as when the carpenter mentions with just the right touch of consternation that a man has just been carried dead to church whom 'last Monday' he saw at his work.

Most important of all, the characters are not pale shades, or types, as they are in the analogues. Alison is not simply the type of a lustful and unfaithful wife. Chaucer avoids the mistakes of the analogues. One analogue makes her a prostitute. This loses all the comic capital of the deceived husband and the need for secrecy. In another, she intends to receive three lovers in succession, which degrades a story which in any case is necessarily poised on a precipice above a slough of mere grossness. Chaucer's Alison is described with the same care as that with which he described the Duchess Blanche, though with infinitely greater art, and to vastly different effect. Thus she has the conventional and fashionable beauty of a white forehead, but this is how Chaucer praises it:

Hir forheed shoon as bright as any day
So was it wasshen whan she leet[1] hir werk.

I (A), 3310–11

She wears an apron white as morning milk, plucks her eyebrows, and has a lecherous eye; she sings like a swallow (!),

She was a prymerole,[2] a piggesnye[3]
For any lord to leggen[4] in his bedde,
Or yet for any good yeman to wedde.

I (A), 3268–70

There never was 'so gay a popelote or swich a wenche' (both of these are 'low' words). She is, if we may be permitted the twentieth-century equivalent, a village popsy, with a well-washed, luscious, vulgar (and genuine) allure. Chaucer does full justice to the allure as he does to the vulgarity. She is a comic figure to the courtly audience, and to us because our eyes by Chaucer's art are adjusted to his vision of her. She is amusing in action by descriptions such as that of her hoity-toity air (no more) when Nicholas begins his rough and direct wooing and by her speedy capitulation; by the way she struggles when firmly in his grasp, and promises only to cry out in the future.

The portrait of Absolon is painted with similar amused care and satire. The village-clerk and barber, he is a dandy, according to his lights, with a high-pitched voice and affected accent, and is 'somewhat squeamish'. He is, of course, an amateur actor, and fancies himself with the women. Had he lived in the present day he would doubtless have been brilliantined like a cricket-hero, and have flaunted a big tie with a bathing-beauty pattern on it. As it was the fourteenth century, he had to be con-

[1] finished.   [2] primrose.   [3] a dear little thing.   [4] lay.

tent with the pattern of St. Paul's windows cut on his shoes.

The character of the old husband is as remarkable for what is left out as for what is put in. Great care is taken to make him a clear, but decidedly background character. Thus we are briefly told of his age and jealousy. We see his blend of respect and contempt for Nicholas's learning, his simple conceit of the practical man. We are made aware of his unthinking piety and clumsy good intentions. This is sufficient to make him real enough for the stratagem to have point, but not enough to make us think in terms of real life about the true pathos and bitterness of his situation. A story such as this has to be told without forcing us back on our normal moral feelings. Adultery in real life is too much a cause of suffering and evil. We must not consider the husband too sympathetically. If he, especially, of all the characters is intimately realized, the comedy will become tragedy. This kind of comedy depends on limitation of view, and all the characters are carefully controlled. The *Miller's Tale*, for all its realism, is not real life. It is comic fantasy, and we may adopt towards it the sentiments of Charles Lamb towards Restoration Comedy:

> I confess for myself that (with no great delinquencies to answer for) I am glad for a season to take an airing beyond the diocese of the strict conscience—not to live always in the precincts of the law-courts—but now and then, for a dream-while or so, to imagine a world with no meddling restrictions . . . I am the gayer at least for it; and I could never connect those sports of a witty fancy in any shape with any result to be drawn from them to imitation in real life. They are a world of themselves almost as much as fairy land.

Yet one question remains to be faced—is the *Miller's Tale* poetry? There is no reason why the comic should not be as poetical as the serious. Mr. Berenson coined the useful word 'life-enhancing' to explain the fundamentally mysterious appeal of painting. The same word may be employed for all the arts, and for none more than the poetry of Chaucer. In narrative poetry, as with dramatic, the poetic delight lies partly in the aesthetic pleasure aroused by the formal qualities of the story itself —the interrelation of cause and effect, character and action. There is delight also in the creation of situation, character and setting, whereby our experience of life is enriched; we see more of the world, and, it may be, understand more, through the medium of the imagination. Added to these is the pleasure of hearing vivid speech in metrical form, which may be compared for its fascination to the spectacle of the wide waters of a lake dashing down a narrow gorge in which they find both outlet and restraint. The *Miller's Tale* is rich in all these pleasures. Unless it is asserted that only a restricted number of thoughts and emotions are allowable to be expressed in poetical form, the *Miller's Tale* is poetry. It is, moreover, perfect, as greater poems, say the *Troilus* or the *Knight's Tale*, are not. There are no lapses into frigidity; no inharmonious shifts into another mood.

The tale takes its place in the larger comedy of the pilgrimage in that it grieves the Reeve, who being a carpenter himself, takes to heart the misfortune that befell him of Osney. The Reeve falls into a self-pitying monologue of commonplaces about old age, spoken in a slightly Northern accent suitable to his Norfolk background. But the Host urges on his tale—they are already at Greenwich (Chaucer's place of residence) 'where many a rascal dwells'. The Reeve then tells his tale of how a thieving miller is cuckolded by a Cambridge man from King's Hall (now merged into Trinity College).

The *Reeve's Tale* is told against the Miller, but it is no contrast to the latter's tale; it is a jewel fit to be set beside its peer. It abounds in the same kind of felicities. In both tales Chaucer, apart from his many other superiorities over the writers of the analogues (including Boccaccio), is very much more humane. Neither tale is sordid; in neither tale are the young men and women mere ciphers of lustfulness. Even Alison has to be wooed, while between the miller's daughter of the *Reeve's Tale* and her lover there is a genuine, if somewhat rapidly-sprung affection. There is even a touch of pathos, albeit comic pathos, in her farewell, which includes the surreptitious return of the stolen grain in the form of a huge cake.

The two tales are not precisely the same in quality. The *Miller's* is a comedy about love-making; the *Reeve's* is a comedy of pride and trickery. The sexual element enters into the latter because the miller's pride is tenderest there—he is hit where it hurts most. Although his and his wife's social pretensions are amusingly laid bare, we are conscious less of particular social satire than of a general human satire. Finally, although there is some knockabout farce in the *Miller's Tale*, it is not quite such uproarious fun as the fight in the miller's bedroom in the *Reeve's Tale*.

The pilgrim-Miller's reaction to this tale is not told. It is the Cook who chimes in next, almost beside himself with joy at the *Reeve's Tale* and enthusiastically determined to cap it with one of his own. This begins most promisingly with a description of the wild habits of a London apprentice called Perkyn Revelour which aptly illustrates how the interests of Court and City mingled in Chaucer's audience.[1] We seem to be starting that

[1] One of Edward III's executors was a merchant. The great merchant family of the de la Pole's of Hull became Earls of Suffolk early in the fifteenth century.

comedy of City life which Chaucer could have written so well. But alas, he never wrote it, for the *Cook's Tale*, hardly begun, finishes abruptly, though strikingly. Perhaps three such tales in a row would be too much of a good thing. Chaucer never made up his mind as to what should follow the *Reeve's Tale*, and the whole Fragment ends here.

The next block of stories[1] begins with the curious Introduction to the *Man of Law's Tale*. There are several puzzles here. Why does Chaucer give a list of the contents of the *Legend of Good Women* through the mouth of the Man of Law—especially as it is a list different from the tales he had actually written? Then the Man of Law condemns two stories about incest. Chaucer's dislike of tales about such 'unnatural abominations' was probably genuine, and a similar fastidiousness appears elsewhere in the *Tales*, but is this passage merely a hit against his friend Gower, who had recently written these very stories? Again, why? The Man of Law promises to speak in prose, but as mentioned earlier, the *Tale of Melibeus*, perhaps first assigned to him, was transferred to Chaucer. The Invocation which is the Lawyer's Prologue has nothing to do with his story of Constance, to which it makes hardly more than a grammatical bridge —a lack of unity reminiscent of Chaucer's earlier work. The whole Introduction cries aloud the lack of revision.

Not so the Tale. It is written with care and elabora-

---

[1] The contents of the next Fragment are in some doubt. It certainly begins with the *Man of Law's Introduction and Tale*. Chaucer seems not to have finally decided which tale should follow, as appears from the variants in the Epilogue to the *Man of Law's Tale*, and the omission of the Epilogue itself from many good manuscripts. He may well have decided that what is now the *Shipman's Tale* should follow, but he never made the necessary alterations. I shall assume with Skeat that the *Shipman's Tale* was indeed meant to follow, and with it the whole sequence of Group B, as much from the convenience of this arrangement as from conviction that it is right.

tion. The 'matter' is a pious tale of folk-lore origin, which Chaucer read in the Anglo-French of Nicholas Trivet. He translates the story straightforwardly, enriching it as he did the *Troilus* with his own understanding of how such things could come to be, and with his own vivid evocations of speech and scene, his own pity for suffering. These rhetorical embellishments arise naturally enough from contemplation of the 'moving accidents' of the story. But in this tale in contrast with the *Troilus*, there are only two places where Chaucer is inclined seriously to suspect that his source may be mistaken, both marked by the doubting phrase 'Som men wolde seyn' (II (B), 1009 and 1086), where Trivet is in fact quite unequivocal. Both these examples refer to minor details which seem to Chaucer not to be in accord with what would have been expected from the characters concerned. This caution is the more striking in that the tale as a whole is of the kind of impossibility that pious legend delighted in. It tells of Constance, daughter of the Christian Emperor of Rome, who is twice married to a pagan king, twice converts her husband, is twice betrayed by her irreconcilably pagan mother-in-law, and twice committed to the sea in a boat without oars or sails. In each case she is afloat for several years. Her first husband is killed by his mother but she is eventually restored to the second. The artistic weakness of such a plot is obvious enough, but Chaucer handled it in the fullness of his powers. He accepts the miraculousness—he is not misled by his capacity for realizing detail into giving, as for instance Trivet does, a list of stores for a three-year voyage. He sees it as a Miracle of the Blessed Virgin, who supported Constance in her trials. He comments now and again on the vicious men and women who so afflict the pure and gentle Constance, taking the material for these comments from the *De Contemptu Mundi* which he had recently translated. At the same time a miracle was not fantasy to Chaucer; he believed the story. He sees the action very vividly in its time and place. The diplomatic overtures for a state marriage (which he must have known so well); the geography of the seas around England; the state of languages in England in about the fourth century; the usage of Courts; the felicities of home—all this and much more is suggested or described. Even more notable, as we should expect, are the very great beauty and intimacy of the description of Constance. There is perhaps nothing more exquisite in all his work than the passage, entirely his own, where Constance for the second time is to be abandoned to the sea, on this occasion with her baby. We see the very movement of her hand as she draws the kerchief off her own head to put it on the child; another phrase tells of the large crowd following her, sympathetic, but silent and helpless. Her prayer is the most moving of all, where she asks pity for her child from that Mother who saw her own Child torn on the Cross, with whose woe the woe of no man can stand comparison. Withal, the world of Constance is the same world as that of the *Troilus*. The same stars, the veil of pagan mythology reft aside, govern human affairs under God. The poem is fully astrological as well as fully Christian.

The *Man of Law's Tale* is not, of course, in the same class as the *Troilus*, the *Miller's Tale*, and several others. The beauty of the tale lies in the character of Constance, her love, faith and fortitude, and the pathos of her sufferings. The plot provides too weak a foundation for any very complex structure to be built upon it. It is repetitious, but does not develop. There is room only for

Constance's single noble virtue, and that itself cannot grow, or produce more than one perfect bloom. The realism of settings scattered to the ends of the known world cannot add up to a convincing picture of a unified social and spiritual environment. Minor characters appear too briefly for them to develop in any fruitful relationship with Constance. There is no interwoven web of character and action, motive and event. The tale is not a failure—Chaucer has worked too carefully upon it for that —but its own limitations allow it only a restricted flight.

A 'thrifty' (profitable) tale, the Host calls it, and at one time, at least, Chaucer intended to follow it with the contrast of the *Shipman's Tale*, an amusing worldly anecdote told in an amused, worldly way without implications of any kind, of how a monk tricks a merchant's wife, and the wife keeps even keel by tricking her husband. Chaucer as usual clothes the skeleton of the plot in warm flesh and blood, and fourteenth-century clothes and manners as well. We see the merchant busy in his office, and the free and easy monk coming and going from monastery to garden, house, board—and bed. There is no satire, but some incidental irony. The tale was never properly revised for the Shipman, but is told by a woman. It has the peculiarity that it begins with a condemnation of festivities and expense by one who rejoices in both. This curious blend is reminiscent of the Wife of Bath, whose Prologue as it were plays on the same sort of theme in a major key.

After the *Shipman's Tale* the mood is again changed through the medium of the Host's words. He gently and respectfully prays the Prioress to tell them a story, to which she freely and courteously agrees. Her Invocation to the Blessed Virgin establishes the mood of pious exaltation in which the tale is both told and heard.

(In his many prayers, especially to the Virgin, Chaucer blends a joyful lyricism with splendour of thought and of diction, as he does nowhere else. Humility and exaltation, simplicity and magnificence, go hand in hand.) The tale catches perfectly the sweetness of Mother with Child, the charm of little children, the devouring misery of anxious motherhood. It ends in a glory of devout wonder and gratitude at the miracle. Though brief it is perfectly proportioned—as much a gem of flawless artistry as the *Miller's Tale*. It is an irony which was certainly not realized by the poet, that the gentlest of all the pilgrims should tell what is, from a point of view impossible to the Middle Ages, the only cruel and fanatical story of them all.

Every pilgrim is affected by the pathos and devotion which shine through the *Prioress's Tale*, until the Host begins his jocular address to Chaucer. We are reminded of the Eagle in the *House of Fame*. The poet's plumpness is still good for a joke, and the old charges are brought against him—that he is abstracted and aloof from his neighbours. And again as in the *House of Fame*, Chaucer in reply represents himself timid and ignorant, this time of any poetical art, for he tells what is, within the drama of the *Tales* themselves the *only* failure—a pleasant irony indeed! But it is very characteristic of his subtlety that this failure is in fact cover for both literary and social satire. The satire makes the poetry here, and gives the verse its meaning, for if the tale were really a failure to us, the real audience, it would be a silly joke indeed.

Chaucer's Tale of Sir Thopas contains a certain amount of farce; a good deal of satire of tail-rhyme romances of chivalry; and a good deal of satire of the Flemish Knights. To appreciate the farce it is necessary only to be human; for the rest, the nearer one is to the inner knowledge

K

of a courtier in Chaucer's circle, the more easy it will be to appreciate the joke. One of the main appeals of humour of this kind is that one should be 'in the know'; should be modish enough to recognize old-fashioned clichés in verse, or unfashionable habits. The poet parodies what is already thought to be absurd, by describing it with ridiculous exaggerations and additions. It is in the felicity of this creative caricature that the poetry exists, and Chaucer has created an absurdity of a knight in Sir Thopas, which any one can recognize, however ignorant of tail-rhyme romances and Flemings.

From Chaucer's mocking of knight-errantry here, and from his cynical reference to 'the book of Launcelot de Lake, That wommen holde in ful gret reverence' in the *Nun's Priest's Tale*, it may be guessed that Chaucer had little respect for Arthurian knight-errantry, though plenty for Knighthood as a Christian and crusading order. His scepticism is notable in an age when the English were remarked upon for their belief in Merlin and Arthur. One wonders what he thought about the Arthurian inspiration of the Order of the Garter. His rejection (if such it be) of Arthurian legend is an interesting example of his scepticism, of his capacity to think for himself, as well as showing one important direction in which his tastes did *not* lie.

When the Host stops the doggerel of *Sir Thopas*, Chaucer is plaintive but docile. He chooses to tell instead a 'moral and virtuous tale', and goes on to discuss the verbal differences between the Gospels, mainly, one suspects, to sober down the mood, for his only ostensible reason is thus to excuse any verbal differences between the forms of the proverbs he uses, and those his audience know. But the proverbs also are important, for the *Tale of Melibeus* which he proceeds to relate is crammed full of them, and they are used, as he says, 'to enforce the effect of the matter'. Chaucer calls this long prose translation a 'little' thing, more modestly than accurately. It is certainly not meant to be funny. It is a serious discussion of various ethical problems. It is sensible, moderate, sober, understanding, and Chaucer had every reason for respecting it as he must have done to have felt it worth translating. The *Melibeus* is out of date now, but full of interest to anyone who will read it with the historical imagination. There is a thread of story, and some obvious allegorical interpretations arising from it. But the main body of the work is debate, the balancing of conflicting authorities often summed up in the pregnant scraps of common sayings, the 'crystallized thought' of proverbs, which are typical of Chaucer and his age. The topics discussed are the worth of women, the justice and injustice of war, true friends, flatterers, the fickleness of 'the people', the need to love God, obey the law, etc., etc. The *Melibeus* is a most useful collection of the common opinions of well-educated pious people. We are harassed by the same troubles as were they. We do not see our problems in the same light—but that is due to historical change. Where we tend to see the working of blind mass forces, they saw many human persons making mistakes and committing evil deeds. A humble reading of the *Melibeus* will teach us more of Chaucer's poetry, of man, of moral evil and of good (at any rate as seen in the fourteenth century) than any number of impulses from a vernal wood.

The Host is too bursting with his desire to say how different his own wife is from Prudence, the wife of Melibeus, to comment on the tale. And indeed comment would only remind us of the extreme unrealism of this long prose treatise delivered on the way to Canterbury.

The joke of the masterful man mastered by his wife is an old and good one, but as we do not know what the real Harry Bailly's wife was really like, we cannot tell if the humour lies in the truth or the falseness of the description of her; it might be either. At all events, the Host's remark provides welcome relief after the ponderings and ponderousness of the *Melibeus*. Chaucer may have introduced this new element in the Link because he was abandoning the well-used device of contrasting tales. The Link itself provides the contrast both to the preceding and to the following tale. The description of the Host's termagant wife also underlines one of the themes of the *Melibeus*—the relationship between husband and wife—which becomes more and more prominent as the *Tales* proceed. At the moment, however, it is the Monk whom the Host calls on for a tale. He answers the Host's half-saucy, half-respectful sallies stiffly enough, and embarks upon a series of solemn Tragedies, telling 'the harm of those who stood in high degree' and fell.

By far the best of these accounts is the story of the death of Count Hugelino of Pisa and his three children, taken from Dante. Chaucer's love and understanding of little children and of parental devotion make this an exquisitely pathetic little piece—Dante's sombre power turned all to favour and to prettiness. Most of the other examples are too bare to be moving. They illustrate a commonplace theme and if anything induce a feeling of gloomy satisfaction at seeing it so widely exemplified. The subtle modern conception of tragedy as an ennobling spectacle was of course far from the medieval mind. The *Monk's Tale* mingles classical legend, classical history, biblical history, patristic legend, and modern instances.[1]

[1] Such a mixture is sometimes mistakenly thought to be a special characteristic of Renaissance writers.

They all have the same historical validity whether found in poetry or chronicles, whether old or new, read or heard of. This does not mean that Chaucer, Boccaccio (for the *Monk's Tale* is modelled upon a Latin work of his), and the men of their time were fools who could not tell fact from fiction. They well knew the difference between *historia* and *fabula*. But because they inherited less knowledge than we, they drew the line between fact and fiction less strictly and in a different place.

The Knight himself cuts short the *Monk's Tale*, although originally Chaucer perhaps made the Host break in, and later substituted the Knight for him so as not to duplicate the interruption of a story by the same person. As with *Sir Thopas*, the interruption is a dramatic device. The story has gone on long enough for Chaucer's purpose, but it would be absurd to think that he himself thought it bad as far as it goes.

The next tale is a delightful contrast to the *Monk's Tale*, and one of the most perfect humorous tales that Chaucer ever wrote. He reduces the well-known beast-fable of the cock who is beguiled by the fox but saves himself at the last minute, to the barest narrative essentials, and fills out this apparently unpromising frame with the most delightful variety of description and learned commentary, all conceived in a matchlessly comic vein. The tale is told by the Nun's Priest, whose character is too briefly sketched for it to have any significant relationship to his story.

As is usual with the comic tales, the fantasy of the plot is played against a setting humble, realistic, contemporary and local; in this tale, the tiny smallholding of a poor widow. The cock of her poultry-run is a most learned cock, especially in the favourite Chaucerian fields of dream-psychology, medicine, and astrology. He is very ready to discourse on all these subjects, while in

later times painstaking scholars have been no less ready
with laborious learning to check and pronounce him correct. It becomes such a learned cock to outdo in splendour all other fowls;

> Lyk asure were his legges and his toon.
>
>   B 4052; VII. 2862

His body, like his speech, is a blaze of colours.

It is a comic device inherent in the beast-fable to make
a bird talk like a learned man and then to show it going
off to have a dustbath, but it has never been better done
than here. The *Nun's Priest's Tale* is genuine comic
poetry, a comic image of life itself. When Chauntecleer
the cock swaggers up and down the farmyard before his
seven adoring wives, the description reflects both animal
and human nature; it has the poetic vitality of metaphor.
We see a man in the bird, and the bird in men. The
truth and the absurdity of this double vision, where each
aspect throws light on the other, create comic poetry at
its best. When Chauntecleer shudders with delight at
being flattered by the fox, Chaucer not only gives us a
superb visual impression of the way a bird flutters its half-
closed wings; he most powerfully suggests the reactions
of a certain type of person when flattered. Dame Perte-
lote, Chauntecleer's chief and most beloved wife, pooh-
poohs her husband's odd ideas with an amusingly wifely
briskness, and shows an almost motherly concern with
the state of his health and bowels. Chauntecleer patron-
izes his less learned lady with husbandly smugness, and
shows an equally characteristic irritation at being told
to take medicine.

Good as these characters are, the great joy lies in the
general presentation of the tale, with the full panoply of
the author's learning and rhetoric. Nearly all the sub-

jects of Chaucer's most serious thought are here. The comedy is in the neatness of the disproportion. Chaucer plays with serious ideas; while pretending to treat his frivolous 'matter' seriously, he treats serious matters frivolously. Thus he ponders yet again the problems of predestination and foreknowledge, but they arise out of the concern of a farmyard fowl who has dreamt about a fox. This does not mean that he is satirizing concern with the problem of predestination, but that it was so much a part of his thought that he enjoyed it whether serious or light-hearted. The nearest parallel in English literature is the exquisite *Rape of the Lock*, where Pope enjoys himself by using frivolously the same heroic convention which he also enjoyed as serious literature. This kind of joyful burlesque is the play of the mind. The mind takes the same kind of exercise for pleasure, without concern for ultimate causes, as it normally takes when seriously at work. The prime example of this kind of play in this poem is Chaucer's use of rhetoric, which again, may be compared with Pope's playful use of rhetoric in the *Rape of the Lock* and the *Dunciad*. Too many critics have considered that in the *Nun's Priest's Tale* Chaucer, now free from the bonds of rhetoric, is satirizing its feebleness. Nothing could be further from the truth. Chaucer always used rhetorical devices, though he certainly became more adept in their use as he grew older. He laughs at the rhetorician Geoffroi de Vinsauf in this poem because he is a poor poet—and that is humorous enough in a man who claims to teach the art of poetry. But Geoffroi did not own the art of poetry: he was only one among several who passed on certain rules of composition, which were enshrined in a tradition far greater than he. It would be unfortunate if every critic were to be scorned because he wrote poor poetry, even though the verse of such critics is fair game to any poet or satirist. Chaucer in the *Nun's Priest's Tale* is writing comedy, of which the essence is disproportion. He uses the high 'sentence' of rhetoric, properly to be employed only, as everyone knew, on a high subject, to adorn a low subject. Children make a similar joke when they dress up a dog in human clothes. The dog himself, the clothes themselves do not make us laugh: it is their conjunction which is comic.

The themes of Chaucer's serious thought—dreams, love, predestination, and the rest, are here all turned to comedy and cheerfulness. It is great self-assurance that allows a poet the strength to relax his grip on his most cherished thoughts and convictions in order to juggle with them and catch them again. And with this tale we come to the end of the extraordinarily brilliant sequence of the second group.

Following Skeat's order we come next to Group C containing only the *Physician's* and *Pardoner's Tales.* (Robinson, Fragment VI.) There are no connections at beginning or end, and the two tales may have been meant to come anywhere. With so much richness about, the relatively poor *Physician's Tale* must be hastily dealt with. It is no 'fable' but a 'storial' thing, says Chaucer; in other words, it is true. The ultimate source is the historian Livy. The story is dressed up as usual. Nature appears briefly, there is another condemnation of feasts, and an address to governesses. There is one fine scene, of the death of Virginia. But the formula fails. It is easy to see why. The rhetorical dressing is not sufficiently related to the body of the subject; characters, motives, actions, are not sufficiently interwoven, and the style is often drab. There are good passages, but they do not add up to a poem.

The Host, however (and presumably Chaucer too), does not think so. He swears 'as if he were mad' at this further example of Chaucer's interest in the sad fates of true and beautiful women. Unless he hears a merry tale straight away, he will break his heart for pity. The Pardoner is very willing to oblige, if he can first get a drink.

Perhaps the draught of moist and corny ale goes to his head, for with a leer he reveals all the cunning tricks by which he cheats simple folk of their money, preaching against avarice in order to feed his own. There is no evidence, however, that he is drunk, and there is a very similar self-revelation by a villain in the *Roman* (English *Romaunt*, 6135 ff.). It is a familiar method for a medieval satirist to have a villain describe his own·tricks, and the apparently impartial Chaucer is fond of letting his characters expose themselves out of their own mouths. There seems to have been a tradition that some kinds of villain shall declare themselves, which perhaps derives from the stage, and lasts at least till the seventeenth century. Iago, Richard III, Edmund the Bastard are among the more distinguished examples. The Pardoner goes on to preach the kind of sermon he usually preaches: first, he speaks against various vices, then tells an extended *exemplum* of how three treacherous and debauched men sought Death in their drunken arrogance—and found it. The actual tale is short, and no sooner finished than the Pardoner not only reverts to his homiletic vein but, by a magnificent twist of irony, is made to appeal to the Pilgrims to buy those very relics he himself has earlier so shamelessly exposed. It needs the harsh crudeness of the Host's reply to express something of our feeling towards this cynical and depraved creature, and the Host gives him full measure. Even so, Chaucer will consign none of his pilgrims to outer darkness; the Knight comes forward as

peacemaker, and the Host and Pardoner kiss in reconciliation.

Chaucer is economical. The depth of the satire on the
Pardoner lies in the excellence of the morality of his tale.
Not many satirists manage to convey their love of the
good as well as their hatred of the bad. Chaucer's satire
never seems to spring from personal spleen. The satire here
is balanced and deepened by the irony of the situation,
where the Pardoner preaches what he does not believe but
ought to believe, and enforces the moral lesson in-
advertently by the very example of his own shamelessness.

The tale itself, apart from the homiletic passages, is
told almost entirely through excellent dialogue. Slight
as it is, it has a touch of awe, even of horror, found nowhere else in Chaucer, as we watch the three criminals
rush on their fate. The most striking figure is that of the
mysterious Old Man who walks the earth, poor and
longing for death, knocking with his staff upon the
ground which is his 'mother's' gate, crying 'Dearest
mother, let me in'. This strangely haunting character
seems to be largely Chaucer's own invention. He is the
weariness of old age incarnate. Yet Death takes the
young rioters, who have questioned the old man so
rudely to discover where they may find death. A sense
of the ineluctable mystery of life lies beneath the simple
plot. There is not often this profundity of suggestion in
the *Canterbury Tales*.

We now come to a new section, a large one, since it
may reasonably be held to be composed of Groups DEF
(III, IV, V). We plunge straight in.

> Experience, though noon auctoritee
> Were in this world is right ynogh for me
> To speke of wo that is in mariage.

III (D), 1–3

And indeed the Wife of Bath's theme (for it is her cheerful, arrogant voice we hear) is tribulation in marriage—
particularly the misery she has caused her five successive
husbands. Chaucer draws on the anti-feminist literature
of an anti-feminist age as material for his supreme feminist
to use in her assertion of female rights, and her very
assertion is a superb satire on women. Imagine being
married to the Wife of Bath! Flesh and spirit quail
before her insatiable appetite, her incessant talk, her
joyously predatory vitality. We laugh at her only because, seeing the danger, we know we are safe. While
she was alive the joke was on her husbands: for the rest
of time it is on her, the supreme justification of all the
bad things 'thise olde wyse' have ever said about women.
Her Prologue, a glorious comedy of wifely oppression,
is in a way similar to the Pardoner's in that it is a confession, revealing all the immodest tricks of her successful domination, all her womanly vices. The relation of
her tale to her Prologue is also a little similar, since it
contradicts her professed conviction. Once the husband
in her story had granted his wife what women want most
in all the world—sovereignty—then

> *she* obeyed *hym* in every thyng
> That myghte doon hym plesance or likyng.
>
> III (D), 1255–6

But the Wife goes on to ask—as the Pardoner had asked
for alms—for

> Housbondes meeke, yonge, and fressh abedde
> And grace t'overbyde[1] hem that we wedde,
>
> III (D), 1259–60

—a request which no more arises out of her tale than
the Pardoner's request did from his. The implication of

[1] outlive.

the Wife's tale is that husband and wife should each yield the other the 'mastery'. She is condemned out of her own mouth.

But from our safe distance we love her, as we love the cowardly cheat Falstaff. Her enjoyment of life and of her own successes communicates itself to us. High spirits and laughter are infectious. Far from detecting in her, as do some critics, any underlying insecurity, any near-tragic need for love, we see in her only the energy, luxuriousness, joyfulness, cunning, of the daughter of Mars and Venus. She gladly grants virginity its superior place, but

> everich hath of God a propre yifte,
>
> III (D), 103

and she will envy no virginity in the full and joyful practice of her own gift.

> God bad us for to wexe and multiplye;
> That gentil text kan I wel understonde.
>
> III (D), 28–9

However, she does not love marriage for the joys of the family circle.

Her tale centres on the twofold problem of what women most desire, and what should be the proper marriage relationship. The religious and legal doctrine of the husband's headship of the wife is set against the love-doctrine of obedience to the loved one. With Chaucer these questions are linked with the discussion of what is true 'gentilesse' or nobility, on which there is a long disquisition in the Wife's *Tale*.

> Crist wole we clayme of hym oure gentilesse.
>
> III (D), 117

Great possessions and inheritance do not make nobility, for often we see a lord's son do 'shame and vileynye'.

Poverty is no disqualification for nobility. God chose to live in poverty when he came into the world, and poverty, though hateful, is a good. Age is no disqualification, for both experience and authority command us to respect old age.

The tale is thus subtle and rich in significance. At first, while the character of the narrator is clearly before us, the tone is satirical, and it is women, again, whom the Wife of Bath is made mainly to satirize. Then the tone imperceptibly changes, and the knight is regarded somewhat ironically as he gloomily settles in to his wedding night with the old hag who has saved his life. It is she who instructs him in true 'gentilesse', and her instruction is related to the plot by Chaucer's sharpening of the final dilemma with which she confronts him. In Gower's treatment of the same plot the knight's choice is between having the lady beautiful by day or by night. The knight's choice in the Wife's *Tale* is between having the lady poor, old, and ugly, but humble and true; or beautiful with all the risk that beauty may bring. This is a much more interesting problem. When the knight grants the lady sovereignty by allowing her to make the choice herself, she chooses to be fair, and humble and true as well. Having been granted sovereignty she uses it well and returns it. There is the foundation for a perpetual generous exchange.

In the poem there is, too, a genuine mysteriousness and freshness in the glimpse of the fairy ladies dancing 'under a forest side'. They disappear when the anxious knight approaches, and he finds only the old hag. Chaucer does not attempt, as Gower does, to go into the details of the enchantment; he knows when to leave well alone. The interest of the plot, its relation with the narrator and with other stories and themes in the *Tales*, the grace, humanity and humour of the telling, make the poem one of Chaucer's best.

At the end of this delightful tale the squabble between Friar and Summoner, which has shown itself for a moment earlier on, breaks out afresh, and they each tell a tale against the other, the Friar telling of a Summoner who had to do with a Devil, and the Summoner telling of the discomfiture of a begging Friar by a sufficiently gross trick. Each tale has traces of Northern associations which lead one to suspect private jokes now lost, but which do not hinder appreciation of the poems. Neither friars nor summoners were popular members of society, and they are amusingly satirized—the coarse oppressiveness and stupid arrogance of the summoner: the ingratiating oiliness, the canting hypocrisy and selfishness, the general Chadbandery, of the friar. The setting is vividly realized in each tale, but the Summoner's in particular evokes the interiors of yeoman's cottage and lord's hall with the warmth and solidity, the familiar intimacy, of the Dutch interiors of Teniers. Each tale has further elements of variety—a passage on the ways of devils in the *Friar's Tale*, a short sermon on Ire in the *Summoner's Tale*, both of which are ironically relevant to the plot, and show once again the richness of Chaucer's interests.

From the low-life comedy of Summoner and Friar, Chaucer sweeps us to the graces and stresses of the *Clerk's Tale of Patient Griselda*, not without warnings to the Clerk from the Host against 'high style', and a request for adventures. But the Clerk does not tell about adventures, and makes some moderate use of rhetorical terms, colours and figures.

Something has already been said of the attitude of the age to such stories as that of Griselda, whose patience was so cruelly tried by her husband. It was originally a folk-tale of an otherworld husband, but Boccaccio who first wrote it down made it much more realistic, and Chaucer, working from Petrarch's Latin translation, continued the process. This by now excessive realism inevitably obscures its true affinities, which are with religious myth rather than with human behaviour. The story of Griselda is a story similar to that of Job. It is about faith maintained in the face of bitter suffering, faith in the goodness of the world maintained against all appearances. Shakespeare's last Romances use trivial plots to illustrate this same theme. Jupiter in *Cymbeline* says, as Griselda's husband might have said, 'Whom best I love I cross'. Boccaccio, being given this great theme, reduced it to a trivial plot. Even so, the religious significance was not utterly lost sight of.

Chaucer's additions to Petrarch are all in the direction of greater naturalism, and humanity. Griselda becomes even more charming, human and pathetic; more homely, more sensitive, more motherly. The Duke Walter's relations with his people, the negotiations for his marriage, are more realistic. Each incident of the story is more sharply vivid, the pathos is more beautiful. The net result is that the story, in Chaucer's hands, is even more intolerable, the plot is even more offensive to the human and natural setting, however great the allowances we make, and however we are captivated by incidental felicities of feeling and description. Did Chaucer believe it? He says it all took place in 'olde tymes yore', which makes of it not a 'fabula' but a 'storial thing'. He never withdrew his tender compassion for the sufferings of true and gentle women. But the story imposed a tension on belief, and once finished, it was as if a bent bow was released. His scepticism, his sense of proportion, his love of anti-feminist satire, all withheld during the tale, are suddenly released, to send a deadly shaft of laughter among the emotions he has raised;

> O noble wyves, ful of heigh prudence,
> Let noon humylitee *youre* tonge naille
> Ne lat no clerk have cause or diligence
> To write of *yow* a storie of swich mervaille
> As of Grisildis pacient and kynde
> Lest Chichevache yow swelwe in hire entraille.
>
> IV (E), 1183–8

(Chichevache means 'lean cow', lean because she fed only on patient wives.) In the thirty-six lines of this satirical envoy, which moves as smoothly and easily as any of his poetry, there are only three rhymes. It is an astonishing piece of metrical virtuosity, apart from all else.

The envoy finishes with an injunction to wives to make their husbands miserable, and it is the Merchant, somewhat surprisingly, who takes up this further comment on the 'wo that is in mariage'. Though wedded only two months, he lives in sorrow and care. He will tell no more of his own sorrow, but goes on to tell the tale of the marriage of January and May—the old debauched knight, and the flighty young woman who is seduced by the squire Damian. The seduction is the central episode of the folk-tale plot. It takes place in a tree, and by magic opens the eyes of January, who had been blind. But the wife's quick wit provides an unanswerable excuse. Chaucer has poured all the resources of his art into his description of the characters, the festivities, the discussion of marriage at the beginning, and the discussion of truth and untruth in women between the Fairy King and Queen whose argument gives rise to the final episode of the plot. In this tale there is no question of 'sovereignty'. Nor is there any gaiety. It is told throughout with

irony, and sometimes almost with bitterness. It is no
farce of light love, but a sordid adulterous intrigue
arising out of a sordid marriage. All the characters are
presented without glamour, but the worst is January,
with his nasty old man's lust. Chaucer's technique is
almost that of the Imagists when he describes how:

> The slakke skyn aboute his nekke shaketh
> Whil that he sang, so chaunteth he and craketh.
> But God woot what that May thoughte in hir herte
> Whan she hym saugh up sittynge in his sherte,
> In his nyght-cappe, and with his nekke lene.
>
> IV (E), 1849–53

Whatever sympathy May wins here is lost in the irony
of the speech she makes just before she signals to Damian
to get up into the tree. She weeps at what she considers
January's imputation of her falseness.

> 'I have' quod she 'a soule for to kepe
> As wel as ye, and also myn honour,
> And of my wyfhod thilke tendre flour,
> Which that I have assured in youre hond,
> Whan that the preest to yow my body bond . . .
> I am a gentil womman, and no wenche.
>
> IV (E), 2188 . . . 2202

And with these words she crooks her finger at her lover.

Damian gets off lightest. He suffers all the usual
pangs and is very much the conventional young lover,
goaded on by the stings of love. The details of their
intrigue are so realistic as to include May's necessity of
concealing Damian's love-letter by tearing it up and
throwing it into the privy. Damian, however, is called
no more than a 'traitor servant' in a rhetorical flourish
and is compared to an adder in the bosom. His character
is not of any interest.

L

This joyless story begins with a long passage spoken by January in praise of marriage, obviously conceived ironically in terms of the Merchant's confession. It is followed by a debate between January and his advisers as to whether he himself should marry or not, being now sixty years old and wifeless, and having until then always followed his bodily delight. This sets the tone of the whole story, which almost resolves itself into a study of January and the failure of his marriage without love on either side. The plot itself has the same interest as that of the *Shipman's Tale*, in that in both cases the wife's quick wit gets her out of an awkward corner. But the poem as a whole gives us a glimpse into a corner of society which the poet's unsentimental and scornful imagination floods with a daylight which reveals a good deal that is tawdry. The mythological figures of Fairy King and Queen are a further device for discussing the characters of women, and brilliant as the invention is, they do not bring, nor are meant to bring, anything sweet, bright or playful into the general feeling.

After this powerful and harsh comedy of loveless marriage, it is a relief to turn to the exotic romance of the *Squire's Tale*—once upon a time, in the magic land of Tartary. We are led to expect a tale of love, and would gladly welcome one. Yet somehow, Chaucer's mature imagination seems unable or unwilling to bring itself to plot once more the course of young love. The account of the Falcon's lost love is pale and thin after the superb introductory descriptions of how the wonderful horse of brass came to the court, of the behaviour of the people, and of the court festivities. Perhaps the nearest we shall ever get to a full description of a great fourteenth-century festival at Court is the description here of people high and low buzzing around the new wonders, the music, the orderly bustle of the feast, the wine, the form of dances, the secret interchange of looks, even to the hangover on the following morning. We have continually to speak of the brightness, truth and variety of Chaucer's descriptions, and they are indeed one of the major delights of reading his poetry. He creates and sustains a world of fascinating interest, strange to us now, but retaining the essential power of conviction inherent in truth. He is not a mere recorder of visual impressions; he seizes the inner life and spirit of a crowd of people as only Shakespeare can, among other poets. He has a life-enhancing power of perception.

What is most grateful after the spiritual desert revealed in the *Merchant's Tale* is the high-spirited nobility of temper, courtliness at its best, which is enshrined in the pleasant figure of Canace. She has not revelled the night away,

> She was ful mesurable, as wommen be,

and she rises fresh at dawn

> As rody and bright as dooth the yonge sonne.

When she sees the misery of the falcon (with whom she can converse because of the virtue of the magic ring) she asks her:

> Is this for sorwe of deeth or los of love?
> For as I trowe, thise been causes two
> That causen moost a gentil herte wo;
> Of oother harm it nedeth nat to speke.

V (F), 450–3

This is true 'gentilesse' of temper.

The Squire carries his tale to the end of its second part, finally working up to a formidable list of the things he has yet to tell us. But the Tale is unfinished. Mr.

Coghill makes the happy suggestion that Chaucer's delib-
erate plan was to have the Franklin here stifle the enthusiastic narrator with praise. Delightful as the *Squire's
Tale* is, a continuation of wonders or of the account of
lost love would perhaps have dulled its edge. Furthermore, what we already have is decidedly in the Chaucerian vein; what we are promised, of 'aventures and of
batailles', though doubtless a fair indication of popular
interest, seems never to have been greatly to Chaucer's
own taste.

The courteous Franklin, in his praise of the Squire,
maintains the nobility of temper so happily re-won.

> Fy on possessioun
> But if a man be vertuous withal!
>
> V (F), 686–7

He tells what is perhaps the pleasantest tale in the whole
series, as the *Merchant's Tale* is the least pleasant. The
Franklin's Tale, like the *Merchant's*, is about 'the holy
bond of matrimony', and the attempt of the husband's
squire, consumed with desire yet as much to be pitied
as blamed, to break that bond. The difference lies in the
serenity and courtesy in which the story is conceived,
the noble natures of husband and wife, and hence the
'gentilesse' of their marriage. The tale begins where
the *Wife of Bath's* ended, in the husband surrender-
ing the mastery to his wife, and she restoring it to him
again.

> Heere may men seen an humble, wys accord;
> Thus hath she take hir servant and hir lord,
> Servant in love and lord in mariage.
> Thanne was he bothe in lordshipe and servage.
> Servage? nay, but in lordshipe above,
> Sith he hath bothe his lady and his love;

His lady, certes, and his wyf also,
The which that lawe of love acordeth to.

V (F), 791–8

The praise of marriage, ironical at the beginning of the *Merchant's Tale*, is equally obviously sincere at the beginning of the *Franklin's*. Humanity and decency of spirit pervade the whole story, and there is no happier instance among the many in Chaucer's poetry, of the close compatibility of love and marriage—indeed, of the crowning of love by marriage, according to the 'law of love'. Chaucer thus creates the perfect characters for his tale of the lady Dorigen's rash promise, prompted entirely by her love for her husband, to grant the squire her love if the cruel rocks are removed from the coast. She is the central figure of the story, and it is largely in connection with her that Chaucer 'colours' his 'matter'—for although the good Franklin says he knows no rhetorical or astrological terms, his tale employs a good many of both. As usual, we meet some themes familiar in Chaucer's thought—and none the worse for that—such as Dorigen's pathetic longing expressed in her apostrophe,

> Eterne God, that thurgh thy purveiaunce[1]
> Ledest the world by certein governaunce,
> *In ydel,*[2] *as men seyn, ye no thyng make.*
> But, Lord, thise grisly feendly rokkes blake
> That semen rather a foul confusion
> Of werk than any fair creacion
> Of swich a parfit wys God and a stable,
> Why han ye wroght this werk unresonable?

V (F), 865–72

This is a rhetorical 'colour' arising out of Dorigen's position in the story, it is not here a theme inherent in the tale itself. But that she should express her anxiety in such

---

[1] foresight.   [2] vain.

terms is an indication of her character, and is part of the carefully laid chain of cause and effect that leads to her heedless words to the squire. A speech in such terms also gives weight and breadth to the whole tale.

The squire causes his magicianly clerk to perform the impossible miracle of removing the rocks. Thus the very desire to save her husband from danger is the means of trapping Dorigen into a promise of illicit love. In the tale as told by Boccaccio, the impossible miracle demanded by the lady has no reference to her husband's danger. Chaucer's device is more natural to the lady's character, more profound in irony, more poetical in that it makes a more searching comment on the nature of life. It catches more firmly at mind and heart, is altogether more moving. An ingenious anecdote is raised to a drama of human hopes and fears, of enmeshed motives and events.

The end is worthy of the beginning and middle, for the tangled situation is not cut by a trick, a stroke of wit, or a *deus ex machina*. 'Moral vertu grounded upon trouthe', a high aristocratic sense of honour, the infectious power of 'gentilesse', untie the knot. Dorigen in her honesty reveals her plight to her husband, he in his honour tells her to fulfil the bond, the squire in his courtesy releases her, and the clerk in his generosity forgives the squire his debt. None of these virtuous deeds takes place without full allowance for its pain and difficulty; all the details are precisely told, and the very sums of money involved are faithfully related. Practical life is not lost sight of in ecstasies of elevated feeling.

It is not known how Chaucer would have followed the Franklin's lovely story. It brings to an end another great sequence of tales, and the groups which follow are in comparison little more than snippets. The

Second Nun's Tale of Cecilia is usually taken next. It forms
a fragment with the *Canon's Yeoman's Prologue and Tale*,
and nothing better shows the unity of Chaucer's life
work than this interesting combination. The *Second
Nun's Tale* is early work, not even revised to suit the
teller, while the *Canon's Yeoman's Prologue and Tale* is a
fruit of Chaucer's ripest years, obviously written late
in the *Canterbury Tales* period, and yet firmly attached to
the *Second's Nun's Tale*. They make a piquant contrast.
The *Second Nun's Tale* has already been mentioned—
honest, pious, rather restrained and colourless. The
Canon's Yeoman and his master then burst in with the
busy fluster of sweating men and horses, noisy argument,
and angry passions. The contrast could hardly be more
extreme. Once again Chaucer's fertile versatility
entrances us. The hasty arrival of the Canon and his
Yeoman is a complete surprise—very inadequately
explained by the Canon himself. We suspect him from
the start. The murmurings of his man, and the little love
lost between them further arouse our curiosity and suspi-
cions, until finally, when the Yeoman has taken courage
from his company to speak outright, the Canon flees
for very sorrow and shame.

The *Canon's Yeoman's Tale* has the shape of so many of
Chaucer's poems; an introductory passage is followed by
an anecdote, and rounded off by a comment. This time
the subject is alchemy, of which Chaucer displays considerable though amateur knowledge. Obviously, this
knowledge, like so much else known to Chaucer, was
unlikely to be shared by all his audience. Chaucer makes
poetry of it by explaining it dramatically. He enlightens
the audience by creating a situation where explanation
is natural and necessary; he makes poetry out of information by creating a dramatic personal attitude towards

that information. This is part of the secret of his ability to make mere information not only interesting but poetic; it explains why we are rarely puzzled by the mass of recondite scientific and philosophic information conveyed in Chaucer's poetry from the *House of Fame* onwards. What often puzzles us nowadays is not his unusual knowledge, for that he explained himself, but his usual knowledge, the ideas and conceptions so commonplace that the most ignorant and stupid of his audience knew about them, and which he therefore had no need to explain.

The Canon's Yeoman is bitterly disillusioned about alchemy.

> Whoso that listeth[1] outen[2] his folie
> Lat hym come forth and lerne multiplie.[3]
>
> VIII (G), 834–5

He describes in a few lines the infatuation of men so desirous of the fabled riches to be won by alchemy that they reduce themselves to poverty and ill-health in their mad pursuit—the psychology of the gambler. He drives the lesson home by a wonderful *chiaroscuro* sketch of the experimental shop of his master the Canon—the materials, the explosions, the disappointments, disagreements and arguments of the experimenters. Chaucer obviously takes as great a delight in the list of strange and resounding names of chemicals and processes as Milton and Marlowe do in their lists of exotic and romantic heroes and countries. The Canon's Yeoman after showing the ill-success of his own Canon, then proceeds to tell of the downright trickery of another alchemical Canon, describing a confidence trick which Chaucer seems to have learnt from life. Here the attitude is

---

[1] wishes.   [2] to show.   [3] to practise alchemy.

corrective and warning satire, and the Yeoman—or
Chaucer—is consistently hostile to the 'cursed Canon'.
The narrative of the complicated conjuring trick is a
masterpiece of clarity and ingenuity. The interest and
aesthetic satisfaction normally founded in a shapely and
complex plot are here based on the convolutions of the
confidence trick itself, which is of course related to the
characters of the subtle alchemist and his stupid victim.
We smile at the ingenuity of the trick, and the disappoint-
ment of the dupe (a priest, idle and selfish in his degree,
on whom we need waste no sympathy), but the anecdote
provokes a wry smile, rather than laughter. It is hardly
to be called comic.

The tale is rounded off with a hundred lines of consideration of the pros and cons of alchemy, where it is
Chaucer rather than the Yeoman who is speaking. There
is a characteristic avoidance of an extreme position either
for or against. Alchemy, though never intellectually so
respectable as astrology, was nevertheless a well established and accepted science. Chaucer's objections to it
are not scientific; he is prepared to believe that the
experts are right. In so far as he objects, he objects on
practical and religious grounds. First, it is no good for
the non-scientist to practise alchemy, because he is too
ignorant:

> Lat no man bisye hym this art for to seche
> But if that he th'entencioun[1] and speche
> Of philosophres[2] understonde kan.
>
> VIII (G), 1442–4

And secondly; since, according to Plato, scientists are
sworn not to disclose or write the central secret of their
art, because it is so dear to Christ, that He does not wish
it to be generally known,

[1] intention. [2] scientists.

I rede[1] as for the beste, lete it goon.
For whoso maketh God his adversarie,
As for to werken any thyng in contrarie
Of his wil, certes, never shal he thryve,
Thogh that he multiplie[2] terme of his lyve.

                                        VIII (G), 1475–9

It is almost painful, after the sustained variety and
interest of the earlier great sequences, to find that we are
again, when the *Canon's Yeoman's Tale* finishes, at the end
of another sequence. The following group begins with
the *Manciple's Prologue and Tale*. There is another snatch
of roadside comedy, a quarrel between the drunken Cook
and the Manciple, which is smoothed over by the Host.
The *Manciple's Tale* of Phoebus and the Crow follows.
The story seems not to have caught fire in Chaucer's
imagination, and its treatment is somewhat mechanical.
Its main interest lies in yet further comments on the inexhaustible theme of truth in love, spoken with a directness
unusual in Chaucer. The Manciple says he is a man of plain
speech (this explains his use of the 'low' words, 'wench',
'lemman'), and that there is no difference between an
unfaithful wife of high degree, and one who is poor,

But that the gentile,[3] in estaat above,
She shal be cleped[4] his lady, as in love;
And for that oother is a povre womman
She shal be cleped his wenche, or his lemman.[5]

                                        IX (H), 217–20

This is unassailable truth, even if not quite the whole truth,
and Chaucer, who never approves adultery or promiscuity,
may be taken to have agreed with his mouthpiece. It is a
statement sufficiently forthright to command our respect
for the author who lived in the loose and amorous court
of Richard II. The passage goes on, not very logically, to

[1] advise.   [2] practise alchemy.   [3] noble.   [4] called.   [5] sweetheart.

condemn the 'titleless tyrant'. There is some poetic
energy in these denunciations, though they are not connected very satisfactorily with the plot. The tale ends
with fifty repetitious lines on the wisdom of a still tongue,
which, although relevant to the plot, are hardly poetry.

The *Manciple's Prologue and Tale* is plainly part of the
final sequence, for the *Prologue to the Parson's Tale* begins
with a reference to the Manciple. The *Parson's Prologue*
has the interest of a mistake in astronomy, and a plain
change of plan in the number of stories. It seems almost
certain that the weariness of old age is forcing Chaucer
severely to curtail his scheme. Perhaps, too, it is not
unreasonable to detect in the Parson's condemnation of
both rhyme and alliterative verse the beginning of a
turning away from earthly pleasures in Chaucer himself—
a possible development that was always inherent in his
view of things. But whether this be so or not, the
Parson's condemnation is quite in character.

Some have thought that the Parson has more than a
tinge of Lollardry in him. But the Lollards usually condemned pilgrimages, while this Parson is taking part in
one. However, Lollards and orthodox Christians shared
very similar ideals, although the Lollards introduced
modifications in the doctrine and practice of religion.
There is no suggestion of such heresy in the Parson.

His 'pleasant tale in prose' is a sermon, welcomed by
the Pilgrims, to whom it seemed proper

> To enden in som vertuous sentence.

As with the *Melibeus*, the *Parson's Tale* is the voice of the
age rather than of Chaucer. But Chaucer was very much
a man of his age, and these are also his sentiments, the
groundwork of his belief, his philosophy, his ideas, his
very joy in life. Many of the themes touched on in the

Tales are summed up in this long tract. It teaches the usual Christian doctrine, as understood by the late Middle Ages and applied to the circumstances of life they knew. The Parson reminds his hearers of the Day of Judgment, and the torments of Hell. God orders and controls all things, and a man's first duty is self-mastery. Honours, wealth, delights, even love of family, though good in themselves can seduce him from his eternal destiny. There is a long passage about the Seven Deadly Sins, where many things are held up to condemnation, as 'superfluitee of clothing and horrible disordinat scantness'; great households (such as John of Gaunt's, though Chaucer does not say so); 'bakemeats and dishmeats, burning with wildfire and painted, and castled with paper' (as they were in court festivities), and so forth. The commonplace that Christ is the only source of 'gentilesse' is reiterated. One of many shrewd remarks is that inordinate desire for knowledge or glory may be regarded as a form of avarice. Extortion and oppression are roundly condemned, and while 'degree' is upheld, it is a lord's duty to give his dependants cause to love him. Throughout there is a continual insistence on 'reason'. The sermon is a forthright call to repentance; it pulls no punches, leaves few aspects of life untouched; it is uncompromising, brave and honest. It is too long, but even there it commands a perhaps reluctant respect. And certainly no one can hope to understand the many facets of Chaucer's mind without taking it into account. Its stern attitude to any worldly good which is not sought with an eye to gaining the Kingdom of Heaven must be born firmly in mind when reading the *Retraccioun* which immediately follows, and which is probably the last thing Chaucer wrote. But before considering that, the story of his life while he was writing the *Tales* must be told.

Chapter Eleven

THE LAST YEARS

THE outlines of Chaucer's career after 1386 can be traced clearly enough. Much the same pattern of courtiership and public service is repeated and there is still not a word to be found outside his own writing about his personal feelings or opinions.

Having lived in Kent since 1385 and been free from office since 1386, he presumably devoted himself to his writing and to his duties as Justice of the Peace. Doubtless the exercise of such duties further enriched his knowledge of men. He did not enjoy or endure a stationary tranquillity for long, it seems, for in July 1387 he was granted protection for a year to go to Calais in the retinue of Sir William Beauchamp, although as his name does not appear on the list of Sir William's Controller it is not certain that Chaucer went, or if he went, how long he stayed. Also in 1387 the payments to his wife ceased, and it is probable that she died in that year. Perhaps the loss of her annuity caused Chaucer to live beyond his income, for he began to be sued for debt in April 1388, and sold his crown pension for a lump sum about the same time. Other matters made the first half of 1388 unpleasant. The 'Merciless Parliament', controlled by the barons hostile to the court and Lancastrian factions, sat from 3 February to 4 June 1388, and pursued the leaders of the court party with relentless hostility. Sir Nicholas Brembre, formerly Lord Mayor and one of

Chaucer's Collectors of Customs, who was leader of the Victualling guilds and the most important leader of the court party in the City, was found guilty and executed in February in a barefaced travesty of justice not to be condoned by his own violent and unscrupulous character. Thomas Usk, Chaucer's admirer and also a member of the court party, was executed early in March. After a long and bitter struggle Sir Simon Burley, the principal leader of the court party and one of Richard's tutors, was condemned and executed on 5 May. Richard risked his very throne in his opposition to Burley's fate; his queen is said to have gone on her knees to Gloucester to save him; but to no avail. With him perished three other knights of his party. Truly, 'the wrastling for this world axeth a fal'.

Burley's death seems to have slaked the Merciless Parliament's desire for blood, and the tension of hostility relaxed. Richard had no choice but to lie low and make friends. A year later, in May 1389, Richard made his dramatic gesture of self-assertion, and after ridding himself of some of his main enemies began to appoint some of his own nominees. Chaucer was small-fry, but it may well be that he owed his next official post to Richard's new ascendancy. On 12 July 1389, he was appointed to the responsible position of Clerk of the King's Works. Since Gaunt was not in the country until October of this year, it cannot be to his influence that Chaucer owed the appointment. As with his position at the Customs, the Clerkship was not a sinecure, a reward for mere courtiership. He had general responsibility for repairing and maintaining the Tower, Westminster Palace and other royal buildings, and was granted wide powers to obtain materials, control expenditure, and in some cases to impress workmen. In 1390 he was given a special assignment to erect scaffolding for the jousts at Smithfield, and another for repairs to Saint George's Chapel, Windsor. In the same year he served on a commission led by Sir Richard Stury (another of the court party and one of several of Chaucer's friends who favoured Lollardry). The commission's task was to survey the walls, ditches, bridges and sewers along the Thames between Greenwich and Woolwich. In September 1390 Chaucer was robbed no less than three times in four days. On one of these occasions he was assaulted and beaten, and seems to have lost twenty pounds of the king's money, with some of his own. However, he was forgiven the loss of the king's money. Some critics have found in this unlucky incident a possible reason for his resignation from, or loss of, his Clerkship; but he did not cease to be Clerk until eight months later, on 17 June 1391. A more likely reason for the change is to be found in his appointment, made before 22 June 1391, as subforester of the king's park in North Petherton, Somersetshire. He was apparently appointed by Sir Peter Courtenay, who was Constable of Windsor Castle while Chaucer was in charge of the repairs to Saint George's Chapel. (Sir Peter Courtenay seems also to have been a knight agreeable to the king.) So far as is known Chaucer retained this office to the end of his life, and it was obviously less arduous than the Clerkship of Works. Its value is unknown.

Whatever travelling was required by the subforestership, Chaucer retained his dwelling at Greenwich, which may be the 'sòlytarie wildernesse' of which he complains in the *Envoy to Scogan*. His favour remained strong at court and he received in January 1393 a gift of ten pounds for good service; in February 1394 an annuity of twenty pounds; and in December 1397 the grant of a butt of wine yearly. During these years he often borrowed small sums of money in advance from the exchequer, and in 1398 was sued for debt, though this was an action probably arising out of transactions during his Clerkship, since he was sued by the widow of one of his former subordinates. His favour at court again stood him in good stead, and he was able to obtain letters of protection against this suit for two years. We do not know the outcome of the affair. The chances are that he was not poor, though he may have lacked ready money at times. The dilatory methods of the exchequer (often badly in arrears with payments) and the general shortage of currency in the fourteenth century could easily account for small borrowings.

During these later years Chaucer seems also to have established firmer relationships with John of Gaunt's son Henry, Earl of Derby and afterwards Henry IV. At Christmas 1395 and in February 1396 Chaucer delivered ten pounds to Henry, and received a valuable scarlet robe, trimmed with fur, as a gift. Of course no one at this time thought of Henry as future king. Chaucer had always been associated with the Lancastrian faction, especially through his wife, although his main associates and interests seem to have lain with the court party. Moreover, Gaunt had been much out of the country in the past few years. Now Gaunt had returned, and although Henry had been associated (in the absence of his father) with the baronial party in the year of the Merciless Parliament, he seems, by virtue of his Lancastrian affiliation, to have become by 1396 a member of the new court party in which his father was active. To be loyal to Henry was not yet to be disloyal to Richard. Chaucer's friends Scogan and Bukton (if the latter was Sir Peter Bukton from the Holderness mentioned in the *Summoner's*

Tale) were also close adherents of Henry of Derby[1].

Apart from such of the *Canterbury Tales* as were written in this last decade of the century and of Chaucer's life, there are some minor poems which may belong here. They make a mixed bag. *Trouthe*, *Gentilesse*, *The Former Age*, *Lak of Stedfastnesse*, *Fortune*, all express in varying degrees a keen sense of 'This wrecched worldes transmutacioun', with its corollary that

> No man is wrecched, but himself it wene,
> And he that hath himself hath suffisaunce.

> *Fortune*, 25–6

The *Former Age* is an interesting essay in 'primitivism', finishing

> Allas, allas! now may men wepe and crye!
> For in oure dayes nis but covetyse,
> Doublenesse, and tresoun and envye,
> Poyson, manslauhtre, and mordre in sondry wyse.

> 60–3

The fact that these, like much of Chaucer's thought, are common-places, or that he may often have thought differently about the world, need not detract from their sincerity.

There are also two humorous poems to younger friends, Scogan and Bukton. To Bukton, perhaps on the occasion of his marriage, he writes mockingly of marriage, bidding him 'read the Wife of Bath'. In the *Envoy to Scogan* he asks in pretended dismay:

---

[1] Two other friends of Chaucer similarly had a footing in both court and Lancastrian factions; Sir Lewis Clifford, who brought Deschamps' poem in praise of Chaucer from France; and Sir John Clanvowe, the probable author of the Chaucerian *Cuckoo and Nightingale* and therefore one of Chaucer's literary disciples. Both these were distinguished men and both, incidentally, favoured the Lollards, though Clifford passionately repented before his death.

Hastow not seyd, in blaspheme of the goddes
Thurgh pride, or thrugh thy grete rekelnesse,[1]
Swich thing as in the lawe of love forbode is,
That, for[2] thy lady sawgh nat thy distresse,
Therfore thow yave hir up at Michelmesse?

15–19

He gravely reproaches him, for the god of love may extend his displeasure with Scogan to include those who are 'hoary-headed and round of shape'; once more the image of the portly Chaucer arises before us, now grey-headed. He makes an interesting reference to his poetry

That rusteth in my shethe stille in pees.
While I was yong, I put[3] hir[4] forth in prees;[3]
But al shal passe that men prose or ryme.

39–41

There is a note of tiredness here, but it is followed by a reference to his distance from the head of the stream of grace and honour and worthiness, by which he presumably means the king's court. He says he lives in 'solitary wilderness', 'as dull as death', and desires Scogan to keep him remembered 'where it may fructify' —perhaps in the mind of the king, or of Gaunt, or of Gaunt's son.

The handful of short poems of this period includes also the delicious *Merciless Beute*, in which he commits with exquisite skill the very 'crime' of which he had accused Scogan. After praising the beauty of his lady, and complaining in the usual terms that her lack of pity will be his death, he concludes:

Love hath my name ystrike out of his sclat[5]
And he is strike out of my bokes clene
For evermo; (ther) is non other mene.

[1] rashness.   [2] because.   [3] ventured.
[4] i.e. his Muse, his poetry.   [5] slate.

Sin[1] I fro Love escaped am so fat,
I never thenk to ben his prison[2] lene;
Sin I am free, I counte him not a bene.[3]

A part of Chaucer's personality emerges very clearly from these poems. The low estimate of the world and the consciousness of 'elde that in my spirit dulleth me' forbid neither humour nor that intention of making the best of things as they are which appears in such poems as hint at or ask for some reward from king or princes. There is no repining or self-pity. The requests in *Scogan* and *Fortune* may suggest that by this time Chaucer's active life as a 'working courtier', so to speak, was over. No such poetical requests for favour have survived from his earlier, more active years. It may be that the favours he undoubtedly received are to be associated with these poems.

Towards the end of the decade King Richard became more and more unpopular, while divisions increased within the court party. The most famous of these quarrels was that between Gaunt's son Henry and the Duke of Norfolk, which in 1398 culminated in the abortive trial by combat at Coventry and the exile of both. John of Gaunt died in February 1399, and Richard, who was badly in need of money, confiscated the whole of the huge Lancastrian inheritance. This confiscation, combined with many other acts of extortion and despotism, thoroughly alarmed everybody. When Richard set sail for Ireland in May 1399, complete with minstrels and crown jewels, to crush the Irish revolt, he left behind him his own country ripe for rebellion. When the new Duke of Lancaster arrived in England to claim his rights such numbers of Richard's discontented subjects hastened to join Henry that many had to be sent home again for lack of food. Even Henry's eventual seizure of the Crown

[1] since　　[2] prisoner (Professor Tolkien's suggestion).　　[3] not worth a bean.

did not destroy his popularity for the moment (the
English were a byword to the French for their treachery).
In the last five years Richard had completely alienated the
affections of his subjects from the great lords to the
London rabble, and many of his most loyal and efficient
officers stayed on to serve his successor equally loyally
and efficiently. It must have been a relief to serve a king
more capable and less capricious than Richard, while
Henry's claim to be the true successor of Henry III
together with the façade of legalism of Richard's deposition
were a sufficient sop to the conscience of most. There
can be little doubt, too, that Henry's might helped to
confirm whatever seemed shaky in his right. Richard's
cause attracted few martyrs,[1] and the Revolution was
achieved with remarkably little fuss and bloodshed.
Henry IV was received as king by Parliament on 30 September 1399, being in the official terms which Chaucer
repeats,

> Conquerour of Brutes Albyon
> Which that by lyne and free eleccion
> Been verray king.

Chaucer, an old man as the times went, and with a life-
long association with the House of Lancaster, acquiesced
in the change, and addressed the lines just quoted to the
new king in a poem entitled *The Complaint of Chaucer to his
Purse*, a graceful punning request for reward. There was
nothing servile or unusual in such a poem by a court poet,
and doubtless other courtiers, less talented, were accustomed to make similar requests in plain prose. Such
demands were part of the system by which a great man or

---

[1] Although this does not concern Chaucer, it should perhaps be mentioned,
in order to avoid giving a false impression, that when the first flush of enthusiasm for Henry had faded, along with the immediate memory of Richard's
own unpopularity, there were several risings against the new king.

a king obtained and paid for the services of the retinue which was as necessary to him as he was to his dependants. Henry IV was careful to obtain support wherever he could, and was inclined moreover by policy to foster those arts which Richard had cherished for love. But whatever his motives may have been it is pleasant to record that he speedily granted Chaucer an annuity of forty marks on 19 October and a few days later confirmed Chaucer's former grants from Richard. The ostensible reason for this confirmation was that the earlier letters patent from Richard had accidentally been lost, but Professor French makes the pleasing suggestion that Chaucer was unlikely to have been merely careless. As a practised courtier he may have felt that it would be no bad thing, while Henry was in a giving mood, to have new letters under the new seal.

In December 1399 Chaucer took a lease of a house in the garden of Westminster Abbey. His last recorded payment from the exchequer was on 5 June 1400, and on 25 October 1400, according to the inscription formerly on his tomb, he died. He was buried in the Abbey, and this may have indicated that he was held in special honour by the king, for the Abbey was primarily the burial place of Royalty. (The first commoner to be buried in the Abbey was John Waltham, Richard's Treasurer and Bishop of Salisbury, who had died as recently as 1395. This signal honour was paid to him as a mark of Richard's special regard, and many people had objected.) Unfortunately, the chronicler Walsingham who tells us about Waltham does not notice Chaucer's death, so we do not know what people thought. But it is certain that for some years Chaucer had been recognized in both the English and French courts as the great poet of England.

The final honour (if such it be) of his burial gives a greater, indeed an ironic interest, to the last chapter of all his writing, the *Retraccioun*. This short passage of prose comes at the end of the *Tales*, but refers to the whole of his work, and in it he asks mercy and forgiveness of Christ for just those 'translations and indictings of worldly vanities' which had earned him fame. He revokes them in some detail—the *Troilus*, the *House of Fame*, the *Legend of Good Women*, the *Book of the Duchess*, the *Parliament*, the *Book of the Lion* (now lost), those *Canterbury Tales* which tend towards sin, 'and many a song and many a leccherous lay'. He gives thanks for his translation of the *Consolation*, saints' legends, homilies, and other books of morality and devotion.

There seemed something morbid to the earlier critics about this wholesale and as we feel unnecessary denunciation of the secular works, and they tended to reject the *Retraccioun* as a 'monkish forgery'. Later critical opinion tends to accept it as genuine, and very rightly. It appears in all the manuscripts and is entirely credible as a product of Chaucer's style and thought. Works such as the *Troilus* are not condemned for anything immoral in them; Chaucer's followers united to praise his morality, and the reader may judge of it for himself. Their fault lies simply in their 'this-worldliness'. As death approached, Chaucer's mind reverted to the narrowest and strictest definitions of the good life. The attempts of his mature years to have the best of both worlds, Heaven and Earth, is not unreasonably abandoned, since he must now inevitably lose this present world. That *contemptus mundi* found in the *Somnium Scipionis*, the *Consolation*, and the *Parson's Tale* is no longer contradicted by the experience of glad youth is but confirmed by the experience of painful old age. The contempt of the world produced by a vivid sense of the bliss and eternity of heaven had always been an important element in Chaucer's thought, and the evidence of some of his later minor poems may suggest a hardening in his attitude to the world. Now, with both experience and authority, Chaucer's twin masters, advocating the way of rejection, that way was necessarily chosen.

Sir Launcelot, who was the noblest knight of all the world, and with one exception the most virtuous, ended his days in religious retreat and repentance. There is even a suggestion in Dante's *Convivio* that this was the natural development of a man's life; and indeed in fourteenth-century England an old age of retirement in the shade of a monastery was by no means an uncommon end to life. We must remember, too, the commonplaces of Christian thought accepted by Chaucer; that however good a man's actions, if they are not performed for the sake of God, they shall avail him nothing. If one remembers also the uncomfortable duality of the conception of the world's goodness and badness forced so sharply upon medieval thinking, it may well be thought that to spend one's active days in the world and one's retirement in pious repentance and preparation for death, is a very human and by no means foolish way of resolving the duality inherent in both 'experience' and 'authority'. It was worth while to remember the next life; the conception of Heaven was glorious, and there were terrible accounts of the torments of the damned.

There is therefore nothing that need surprise us about the *Retraccioun*, and no reason to reject it. It is a matter of taste whether one accepts or not the fifteenth-century tradition of Chaucer's death-bed repentance, recorded by Dr. Thomas Gascoigne, Chancellor of Oxford University 1434–44. Repentance there must have been, but one reader at least feels it unlikely that Chaucer left it to the very last minute, while the tradition itself might easily have been suggested by this very *Retraccioun*.

Chaucer's family prospered in the fifteenth century. His son Thomas who had received favours from Richard continued to receive them from Henry throughout a distinguished career. He married about 1394–5 and his daughter eventually became Countess of Suffolk.

Chaucer's poetic reputation also flourished. In the middle of the sixteenth century it was even fashionable for courtiers to 'talk Chaucer'. Only about the eighteenth century did he become thought of as predominantly a comic, even a ribald poet—a view which until recently has helped to obscure the understanding of his genius except for a few such as Blake.

Like all great imaginative writers he has presented us with a recognizable world which appeals, through the imagination, to our senses, to our natural interest in human beings and human situations, and to our intuitions of what is implicit in, or lies behind, human beings and situations. He has given, to quote Lascelles Abercrombie, 'some form of art to the relation between known experience and a conception of originating reality'. The range, variety and precision of his descriptions are a perpetual delight, while few have rivalled his narrative power, his capacity not only for describing but for interrelating places, events, persons and ideas. His method is primarily (though not solely) visual, but his scenes are always significant, aesthetically, socially, morally. He presents a satisfying form and a world which is articulated, patterned. There is always a sense of eternal constants.

Above all, one is conscious, in the end, of a remarkable poetic mind and personality. Amusing, ironical, and satirical, he nevertheless portrays the ecstasies and beauties of love with sympathetic understanding, while the miseries of faithful deserted love always arouse his pity and tenderness. Withal, he is courtly; self-assured enough never to appear to take himself seriously when he talks of himself, impossible to shock. He watches the failings and vagaries of men and women sometimes with seriousness, sometimes with a satirical amusement quite free from rancour or bitterness. His mind is subtle, complex, sophisticated; his manner one of well-bred ease. Perhaps because of this very polish and apparent simplicity, he is more difficult to know intimately than a poet at first sight rougher, less balanced, less tolerant and welcoming, such as Langland. Chaucer does not wear his heart on his sleeve. He is not to be patronized, and even after long acquaintance he is often elusive. He appears not to care to be committed; scepticism is easy to him, and there is something irrepressibly impish in him that often leads him to prick the bubble of the prevailing mood however iridescent and soaring it may be. His humour is partly a defence. It defends his pleasure in introducing himself into his own poems; it carries off the natural emotion of indignation at the wickedness of men. His humour is also an expression of his joy in life. More profoundly, it is also one aspect of that sense of proportion which his temperament and his serious convictions induce. Being convinced of the comparative unimportance of the world and oneself, and yet of the goodness of much of life too, he has cause and freedom to laugh. Because of his balance he rarely sees things in terms of plain black or white. He has also a deeply personal vein of pessimistic melancholy, whence springs the curious paradox of a pessimistic view of the actual world yoked with a religious philosophy strongly tinged with an optimistic determinism.

What Chaucer's poetry does not convey is any proud or agonized interest in his own feelings and ideas; nor does he clarify our doubts for us; nor does he try to convert us, or shame us, or in any way form our opinions. With a few exceptions his poetry lacks the mysterious significances, the rich overtones, which we now tend to make our exclusive demand from poetry. Much that Chaucer gives us we now expect to find mainly in the novel. But literature is a unity superior to the divergencies of its forms. There need be no less pleasure in Chaucer's poetry because it unites what later times have divided. It is impossible fully to enjoy or understand his work with only modern conceptions in mind. But for those who are prepared to take the intellectual and emotional exercise necessary to sympathize intelligently with men who lived so long ago the pleasure and reward of reading Chaucer will be great.

SELECT BIBLIOGRAPHY
BIBLIOGRAPHY
E. P. Hammond, *Chaucer, a Bibliographical Manual*, 1908, is the basic work, to be supplemented by D. D. Griffith, *Bibliography of Chaucer, 1908-53*, 1955, and *The Supplement*, 1957, to *The Cambridge Bibliography of English Literature*, 1940, which bring the information up to 1955. *The Year's Work in English Studies*, an annual publication, continues the account.

LIFE
Early lives of Chaucer are useless. Accurate knowledge begins with *The Life Records*, published in four parts by the Chaucer Society 1876-1900. Information discovered later is noted in the bibliographies, but special mention may be made of J. M. Manly, *Some New Light on Chaucer*, 1926.

WORKS
The only good modern edition of the complete works is by F. N. Robinson, second edition, 1957, though the notes are very much compressed and the glossary inadequate for scholarly purposes. W. W. Skeat's six volume edition of 1894, though still being reprinted, is out of date except for the glossary, which is excellent. The edition of *The Canterbury Tales* by A. C. Cawley in Everyman's Library, 1959, reprints Robinson's text without the notes, but has the advantage of full glossing on the same page as the text, and also of course cheapness. Everyman's Library has also a partially modernized text of the *Troilus*. E. T. Donaldson has recently edited a *Students' Chaucer*, 1959, with regularized Middle English spelling and a valuable commentary. The most popular modernization is that by Nevil Coghill in Pelican Books. D. J. Price has edited *The Equatorie of the Planetis*, 1955.

SCHOLARSHIP
Of many valuable works what follows is only a brief selection. Literary material is presented or discussed in *Sources and Analogues of the Canterbury Tales*, ed. W. F. Bryan and G. Dempster, 1941; J. L. Lowes, *Geoffrey Chaucer*, 1934;

C. S. Lewis, *The Allegory of Love*, 1936; T. A. Kirby, *Chaucer's Troilus, a Study in Courtly Love*, 1940; W. Clemen, *Der Junge Chaucer*, 1938; J. A. W. Bennett, *The Parlement of Fowles*, 1957. A. M. F. Gunn in *The Mirror of Love*, 1951, makes an important re-interpretation of *Le Roman de la Rose*. The general background is described by G. G. Coulton in *Chaucer and his England*, 1908, and illustrated by E. Rickert, *Chaucer's World*, ed. C. C. Olson and M. M. Crow, 1948. W. C. Curry studied *Chaucer and the Medieval Sciences*, 1926. Chaucer's Language and Versification were studied by B. ten Brink. *Chaucer's Sprache und Verskunst*, 1884 (translated by M. B. Smith, 1901), third German edition, revised by E. Eckhardt, 1920. For the non-specialist there is *A Guide to Chaucer's Pronunciation*, by H. Kökeritz, 1954. Most modern editions also discuss Chaucer's language and versification.

CRITICISM

Much criticism will of course be found in the books mentioned in the last paragraph, while the following works are also scholarly. Among many interesting studies are H. S. Bennett, *Chaucer and the Fifteenth Century*, 1947; N. Coghill, *The Poet Chaucer*, 1948; D. Everrett, *Essays on Middle English Literature*, 1955; P. V. D. Shelly, *The Living Chaucer*, 1940; J. Speirs, *Chaucer the Maker*, 1951.

ADDITIONAL NOTE

R. A. Pratt, in *Studies in Philology*, 1956, seems to have proved that in adapting *Il Filostrato* Chaucer was helped by the use of a French prose translation, attributed to Beauveau, Seneschal of Anjou.

Much the best book of Chaucer criticism now available is by C. Muscatine, *Chaucer and the French Tradition*, University of California Press, 1957. B. H. Bronson, *In Search of Chaucer*, University of Toronto Press, 1960, is a fresh and useful survey, corrective of Muscatine in some points.

INDEX